LITERATURE FROM CRESCENT MOON PUBLISHING

Sexing Hardy: Thomas Hardy and Feminism
by Margaret Elvy

Thomas Hardy's Jude the Obscure: A Critical Study
by Margaret Elvy

Thomas Hardy's Tess of the d'Urbervilles: A Critical Study
by Margaret Elvy

Stepping Forward: Essays, Lectures and Interviews
by Wolfgang Iser

Lawrence Durrell: Between Love and Death, Between East and West
by Jeremy Mark Robinson

Andrea Dworkin
by Jeremy Mark Robinson

German Romantic Poetry: Goethe, Novalis, Heine, Hölderlin, Schlegel, Schiller
by Carol Appleby

Cavafy: Anatomy of a Soul
by Matt Crispin

Rilke: Space, Essence and Angels in the Poetry of Rainer Maria Rilke
by B.D. Barnacle

Rimbaud: Arthur Rimbaud and the Magic of Poetry
by Jeremy Mark Robinson

Shakespeare: Love, Poetry and Magic in Shakespeare's Sonnets and Plays
by B.D. Barnacle

Feminism and Shakespeare
by B.D. Barnacle

The Poetry of Landscape in Thomas Hardy
by Jeremy Mark Robinson

D.H. Lawrence: Infinite Sensual Violence
by M.K. Pace

D.H. Lawrence: Symbolic Landscapes
by Jane Foster

Samuel Beckett Goes Into the Silence
by Jeremy Mark Robinson

*In the Dim Void: Samuel Beckett's Late Trilogy:
Company, Ill Seen, Ill Said and Worstward Ho*
by Gregory Johns

André Gide: Fiction and Fervour in the Novels
by Jeremy Mark Robinson

The Ecstasies of John Cowper Powys
by A.P. Seabright

Amorous Life: John Cowper Powys and the Manifestation of Affectivity
by H.W. Fawkner

Postmodern Powys: New Essays on John Cowper Powys
by Joe Boulter

Rethinking Powys: Critical Essays on John Cowper Powys
edited by Jeremy Mark Robinson

Thomas Hardy and John Cowper Powys: Wessex Revisited
by Jeremy Mark Robinson

Thomas Hardy: The Tragic Novels
by Tom Spenser

Julia Kristeva: Art, Love, Melancholy, Philosophy, Semiotics
by Kelly Ives

Luce Irigaray: Lips, Kissing, and the Politics of Sexual Difference
by Kelly Ives

Hélène Cixous I Love You: The Jouissance of Writing
by Kelly Ives

Emily Dickinson: *Selected Poems*
selected and introduced by Miriam Chalk

Petrarch, Dante and the Troubadours: The Religion of Love and Poetry
by Cassidy Hughes

Dante: *Selections From the Vita Nuova*
translated by Thomas Okey

Friedrich Hölderlin: *Selected Poems*
translated by Michael Hamburger

Rainer Maria Rilke: *Selected Poems*
translated by Michael Hamburger

Tolkien's Heroic Quest

Tolkien's Heroic Quest

Robert Rorabeck

CRESCENT MOON

Crescent Moon Publishing
P.O. Box 393
Maidstone
Kent
ME14 5XU, U.K.

First edition 2008.
© Robert Rorabeck 2008.

Printed and bound in Great Britain.
Set in Garamond Book 10 on 14pt and Gill Sans.
Designed by Radiance Graphics.

The right of Robert Rorabeck to be identified as the author of this book has been asserted generally in accordance with sections 77 and 78 of the Copyright, Designs and Patents Act 1988.

All rights reserved. No part of this book may be reprinted or reproduced, stored in a retrieval system, or transmitted, in any form or by any means, electronic, mechanical, photocopying, recording or otherwise, without permission from the publisher.

British Library Cataloguing in Publication data available for this title.

ISBN 1-86171-239-1
ISBN-13 9781861712394

ACKNOWLEDGEMENTS

To the authors and publishers quoted.
To the copyright holders of the illustrations.

CONTENTS

Acknowledgements	8
Author's Note	13
Introduction	15
Preface	17
1 Something of the Man	29
2 Beginning With Beorhtnoth	37
3 Tolkien's Heroic Aesthetic	45
4 A Wellspring of Heroic Enlightenment	63
5 Tolkien's Developing Heroics	71
A Moral Conclusion	99
Appendix	107
Biographical Sketch of J.R.R. Tolkien	123
Notes	129
Bibliography	139

AUTHOR'S NOTE

I wish to thank the professors at Florida State University who oversaw this study: My major professor and director of this thesis, Dr. David Johnson who edited the manuscript, and the two professors on the thesis committee, Dr. Christopher Shinn and Dr. Eugene Crook. I wish to also give a special dedication to Lloyd Alexander (January 30, 1924 - May 17, 2007) for writing me back many times and for writing important and most beautiful stories for young people and people who refuse to grow old, especially his *Chronicles of Prydain*; and to my high school English, Creative Writing, and Lit. Mag. teacher Mr. Scott Zucker who infects all students lucky enough to have him with his boundless passion for the romance of language. I also want to thank Dr. James Paxson, Dr. Diane Stephenson, Dr. Marie Nelson, Dr. Leo Sandgren, and Professor Raina Joines; and another special thanks to my mother and father, and to my grandfather, Professor Robert Cunningham Fadeley.

INTRODUCTION

J.R.R. Tolkien was above all else a philologist, a scholarly linguist and expert on the Anglo-Saxon corpus of poetry. Yet, it is not Tolkien's scholarly work which he is primarily remembered for, but his mainstream success with *The Hobbit* and to an ever greater extent *The Lord of The Rings*. In actuality, Tolkien's scholarly analysis and Tolkien's fiction and creations in the realm of *faerie* are not independent endeavors; there is an intrinsic connection between his two realms of writing: Tolkien's creative works owe a great debt to his insight into the areas of his scholarly study, specifically within his observations on the poem *The Battle of Maldon* and the Middle English poem, *Sir Gawain and the Green Knight*. Not only does Tolkien bring the literary flavor of these works into his fictional creation, allowing his reader to transcend his time and inhabit a pseudo-era like but much unlike the world of the Anglo-Saxon poems, Tolkien also applies to his creative work his observations of *ofermod* within *The Battle of Maldon* and the social/ moral distinction which he interprets within *Sir Gawain and the Green Knight*.

PREFACE

The encompassing claim of this study is that Tolkien operated as a social critic through his fictional writing, and that Tolkien's developing social criticism has its roots in his critical interpretations of *The Battle of Maldon* and *Sir Gawain and the Green Knight*. Tolkien was primarily concerned with the elevation of man-made social systems over a divine and moral law, and he worked to deconstruct such systems as dangerous and flawed ideology that would inevitably lead to the downfall of man. Tolkien's specific interpretations on the corpus of his study reflect directly back upon the heroics and social mechanics he creates for his fictional realm of Middle-earth. This claim is intended to underline the important relationship between Tolkien's scholarly study and creative endeavor in a way which has not yet been fully developed within the literary criticism on Tolkien. What interests this study, then, is how Tolkien's work graduated from fairy-tale based upon Anglo-Saxon poetry, high art in itself, to a more socially relevant medium which helped to shape the attitude of readers since its popular outbreak in the 1960s, yet maintained the Anglo-Saxon social criticism which Tolkien saw in the usage of the term *ofermod*, as well as transmuted *ofermod* to a critique of the threatening power structure Tolkien observed in societies of his day.[1] Within this premise of Tolkien as a developing social critic, this study attempts to show: the background for Tolkien's own heroic æsthetic, the components of his heroic æsthetic, and how that heroic æsthetic is developed and personalized within his writing.

Within *The Battle of Maldon* Tolkien interprets the Old English word *ofermod* as "overmastering pride," and a negative reflection of the heroic leader, Beorhtnoth, whose actions within the poem lead to the destruction of the troops under him and a victory for the Viking forces at Maldon. Tolkien understood the term of *ofermod* as criticism of Anglo-Saxon leaders such as Beorhtnoth, and a reflection upon a larger social dilemma plaguing Anglo-Saxon society: that of a heroic code which placed leaders in the centrality of battle, a precarious position which unnecessarily endangered the welfare of the entire society. Consequently, overmastering pride of brash leaders is seen repeatedly in Tolkien's *The Lord of The Rings* and *The Silmarillion*, but where Tolkien begins to come into his own is when he moves beyond mere repetition of his interpretation of *ofermod* within *The Battle of Maldon* and relates *ofermod* to the desire for absolute power observed within the 20th century while giving answer to such power in the form of a reluctant antihero embodying Tolkien's heroic ideals, such as Sam Gamgee.

In Tolkien's interpretation of *Sir Gawain and the Green Knight*, he saw a distinction of social æsthetic from higher moral ordering by Gawain. Such observation worked to deconstruct the chivalric code of the high Middle-Ages as failed social ideology and placed a divine providence above a social structure. Although the poem is from a later era of English literary history, Tolkien's focus remains specifically on the social implications of the poem and the fallibility of a social leader who accepts flawed social ordering above a higher moral truth.[2] Even more important concerning Tolkien's observations on *Sir Gawain and the Green Knight* is the fact that he focuses upon what he sees as the centrality of the servant figure within the poem, the knight

Gawain, and on the fact that Gawain by the conclusion of the poem is able to discern the ordering of a moral truth above the flawed social structuring of a chivalric code. This important observation as well as Tolkien's interpretation of the term *ofermod* in *The Battle of Maldon*, directed the social criticism of Tolkien's creative works. Specifically, Tolkien used his observations of earlier and later Anglo-Saxon social dilemmas to develop his criticism of dilemmas he saw with modern society and modern social codes.

The focus upon Tolkien's social criticism within this study is an attempt to give immediate validity to Tolkien's sub-created[3] world as both high art and relevant social commentary. Too often the realm of faerie is ignored or discarded by scholars as escapism not relevant to the primary world of literary study. What Tolkien shows, and what is the specific focus of his essay *On Fairy-Stories,* is that the realm of faerie or fantasy does have immediate relevance to the primary world. Tolkien, endeavoring in two fields of writing, the scholarly and the fictional, provides such a connection: his scholarly work is directly applicable to his sub-created world of Middle-earth.

The structure of this study follows the development of Tolkien's social criticism and heroic æsthetic. The study begins by looking at some biographical elements of Tolkien's life and how those elements shaped the creation of Tolkien's antihero, the Hobbit. Looking at the development of social criticism in Tolkien's fictional corpus, the study continues by analyzing *The Homecoming of Beorhtnoth Beorhthelm's Son,* a short play based on *The Battle of Maldon* which helps to show Tolkien's interpretation of the Old English term *ofermod* since within the short play Tolkien is basically reiterating his interpretation of *ofermod* within the Old English poem. The study continues by defining the origins of Tolkien's own heroic ideals and later shows how Tolkien graduated these into his fictional corpus. The study's observations on *Sir Gawain and the Green Knight* are necessarily placed later on, for they represent an important stage in Tolkien's development of social criticism coming after what might be interpreted as Tolkien's recreation of Anglo-Saxon *ofermod* in his fictional work. The study concludes with some direct observations of Tolkien's social criticism at work in *The Hobbit* and several stories within *The Silmarillion*.

Chapter One, *Something of the Man,* begins to develop an analysis of Tolkien's heroic ideals: what attributes Tolkien would uphold within his heroic figures, and why Tolkien held certain values in high esteem. The chapter looks at biographical aspects of Tolkien's life, which will be developed in greater detail in Chapter Three, and positions Tolkien's life at the death of one social system, the Victorian, and the beginning of the modern industrialized and mechanized era. Like the Anglo-Saxon scribes, Tolkien was privy to a time of incredible social change and his writing is a reflection upon and a critique of the changes he saw occurring within his society. By an analysis of Tolkien's *Letters* and *Biography*, the first edited and the second written by Humphrey Carpenter, the chapter sheds light on the personalness and higher social purpose of Tolkien's faerie.

Tolkien was particularly fearful of the absolute power he saw occurring in modernized society. He saw the growth of mechanism and the dying away of religious faith as the growing doom of society. He despised the rape of nature occurring during his time and called for a return to a simplistic society, one penitent and fearful of a higher moral ordering. War also plays an important part in Tolkien's creation; two World Wars shaped disaster into his life, and it was through the terrible destructive power of war that Tolkien found a new critique of *ofermod*. Leaders of Tolkien's time, the modern age, still exhibited *ofermod*, but now they had the power of science and machines, and thus the social damage they could inflict threatened social disaster on a global scale.

In answer to the growing quest for power and dominance of the natural and social world of his day, Tolkien would create his own hero, the Hobbit (Bilbo, Frodo, Sam, Pippin, and Merry). Heroes of a subservient type, the hobbits contrasted starkly with the over-bold conquerors of Anglo-Saxon *ofermod*. With the Hobbit, Tolkien successfully takes the servant figure, which he saw as the truly heroic figure from the Old English corpus,[4] and placed him in the center of the narrative, relegating typical heroics to the outskirts of his fictional creation. With the creation of the Hobbit also came the creation of the anti-quest and the relinquishing of absolute power, power from a realm Tolkien saw as above Man's comprehension. Tolkien's anti-quest is developed in full in *The Lord of the Rings* with Frodo and Sam's journey into Mordor to destroy the One Ring in the pit of Mount Doom.

Chapter One concludes by postulating that Tolkien's heroic code may be analyzed as three basic tenets: respect and appreciation of the natural world, strong homosocial bonds between male figures, and finally a moralistic ordering to his universe, necessarily religious and governed by divine providence; it is Tolkien's religious faith which inspired such depth into his secondary-created world, for he saw his creative act as honoring the Primary World, and adding to that world without trying to manipulate it. Chapter Three looks at each heroic attribute in more depth. Each chapter also looks deeper into Tolkien's biography to discern why he upheld these three tenets, and gifted his hobbits with respect for nature, strong male friendships, and religious piety.

Chapter Two, *Beginning With Beorhtnoth,* positions Tolkien as a social critic utilizing his analysis of the *Battle of Maldon*, specifically in his observation of *ofermod*, or the "brashness of heroes," in his fictional work, *The Homecoming of Beorhtnoth Beorhthelm's Son*, which does little more than repeat Tolkien's interpretations of the Anglo-Saxon poem for the modern reader, but does show the important connection between Tolkien's scholarly and artistic endeavors. As a social critic, Tolkien utilized his analysis of *The Battle of Maldon*, integrating it into his own work, but would not stop there: Tolkien expanded upon his initial interpretation of Anglo-Saxon *ofermod*, gives answer to it in his heroic creation of the Hobbit, and then applies his social model to the modern world.

The study's observations on Tolkien's brief play *Homecoming of Beorhtnoth Beorhthelm's Son*, position Tolkien as a social critic. The play, however, shows Tolkien at a somewhat limited stage of social criticism. The actions and space of Tolkien's *Homecoming* are given entirely to the servant figures, Torhthelm and Tidwald, while the hero, Beorhtnoth, is silenced in death. Tidwald is given Tolkien's voice of social criticism, for he is able to distinguish between social codes of conduct and a higher moral order, a distinction Tolkien was intrigued with and would develop further in his "Tale of Beren and Lúthien" found in *The Silmarillion*, and ultimately in his superlative social reflections in *The Lord of The Rings*. *Homecoming*, however, serves as a good starting point for the study, because of its simplicity and directness of purpose, and also because it shows Tolkien's interest in the servant figure and his placement of the servant figure as central to his narrative.

Chapter Three, *Tolkien's Heroic Aesthetic,* examines the three major elements of Tolkien's heroic code. The first part of the chapter analyzes the complex usage of nature within Tolkien's secondary-creation. There is a duality of purpose in Tolkien's use of nature. Not only is complexly detailed nature imagery central to the success of the believability of Tolkien's secondary world, but like Tolkien's monsters, nature serves as a reflection on society. A society that is in harmony with nature has little to fear from it, but a society that rapes its natural resources and plunders the land is likely to be set upon by chaotic nature personified in monsters. Societies ruled by leaders exhibiting *ofermod* will be set upon by monsters, their ill gained riches taken, and they will be banished from their social center (similar to Hrothgar and Heorot). The delving of the dwarves is a good example of an unlawful use of natural resources, for they are set upon by Smaug in *The Hobbit* and by a Balrog and Goblins in *The Fellowship of the Ring*. Saruman too is set upon by Fangorn and the Ents and Orthanc is destroyed because of Saruman's unruly destruction of the land.

Tolkien's heroes necessarily find peace with nature, both respecting the natural order and furthering that order to its full fruition. Sam Gamgee, Tolkien's ultimate hero, is such a hero who respects nature. He is a gardener and is gifted with magic seeds by Galadriel and with them restores the Shire after Saruman and Wormtongue have scoured it. Nature is not only a component in Tolkien's heroic æsthetic, but provides strong evidence of Tolkien's effectiveness as a social critic, acting as a moral compass distinguishing a moral society from an amoral one.

The chapter continues by looking at Tolkien's homosocial ideal. Tolkien, as an Oxford don, and a recipient of the Victorian ideal of male intellectual superiority, cherished male bonds of plutonic friendship. He was a member of the Inklings, a group of aspiring authors and scholars who met weekly at local pubs to share their writing. Within the Inklings, Tolkien was particularly close to C.S. Lewis, their friendship lasting until the appearance of Charles Williams, whom Tolkien despised because he felt as if Williams' interference ended his friendship with Lewis.

Tolkien's strong homosocial bonds necessarily entered his secondary created world of Middle-earth, but male friendship is not limited to Tolkien's own life experience, rather it is also representative of the influence of the Anglo-Saxon corpus. Bonds between servant and master preoccupied Tolkien, and here again Samwise is a superb example, for his fidelity and plutonic love for Frodo insures the success of their anti-quest, the destruction of the Ring. Tolkien's hobbits, therefore, represent both Tolkien's male friendships and the Anglo-Saxon lord/ servant relationship.

Chapter Three concludes by examining the religious context of Tolkien's work. Tolkien's world is expressly moral and governed by a divine providence, which, in the context of

Tolkien's mythology, ultimately leads back to the divine creator of Middle-earth, Ilúvatar. Tolkien's world, however, is not a mirror of the Christian religion; Tolkien saw such allegorical representation of the primary world as a weakening of his secondary creation, and he strictly keeps religion in *The Lord of The Rings* nondescript. Tolkien had a higher purpose for his fictional world: he was honoring the creator of this world by creating a world of his own, and through his art he was able to add to the primary world without manipulating it. He saw the machines and sciences of the world as manipulating a primary creation which was above man's power to understand, and through his art he gave answer to the industrialized world, and called for a return to an agrarian society, one in honor and in awe of the world, instead of a society that tried to demystify every aspect of God's natural law.

The chapter looks at Gandalf in particular as a Maiar, or helper demi-god of Manwë, chief of the Anar or gods of Tolkien's secondary world. It is specifically heroic of the hobbits to be aware of Gandalf's divine reckoning and his insight and connection with the moral ordering of Tolkien's creation. The heroic in Tolkien's work does not question or delve into the religion of the world, rather it recognizes the moral superiority of certain characters and follows such characters in blind faith. The heroic is in blind service to the divine providence of the world and is intrinsically aware that such providence exists. Tolkien's focus on characters of servitude can again be observed, for not only do his heroic characters follow their lords faithfully, but they follow moralistic leaders (expressly leaders without *ofermod*) knowing without questioning that such leaders are privy to the higher moral ordering of the world. In this context, Tolkien begins to divide moral ordering from social ideology, and, as his commentary on Sir Gawain shows in the next chapter, Tolkien considered it particularly heroic for a character to transcend failed social codes.

Chapter Four, *A Wellspring of Heroic Enlightenment*,

examines Tolkien's W.P. Ker Memorial Lecture on *Sir Gawain and the Green Knight*. In his presentation and examination of the Gawain poem, Tolkien observes that Gawain is particularly heroic because he is able to place higher moral ordering above the failed social æsthetic of his society's chivalric code. Tolkien takes his observations of the Gawain poem and gradually applies them to his own work. Tolkien imbues his character Sam Gamgee with Gawain's special insight, and Frodo, like Gawain, ultimately fails at the end of his quest, but is made more heroic through his human frailty. Also important in Tolkien's observations of the *Gawain* poem is the fact that Tolkien interprets Gawain as a servant figure in faithful service to his lord Arthur. The central narrative of the poem is given over to the servant figure's quest and temptation; thus, here is a text from Tolkien's corpus of study where the major action is given to the faithful servant. Tolkien would expand on the centrality of the servant figure, and develop a layering of servitude, so that gradually the centrality of his narrative would be given over to the servant of the servant, exemplified in Sam's service to Frodo.

Chapter Five builds upon Tolkien's analysis of *Sir Gawain and the Green Knight,* and relates how Tolkien gradually built upon his critical analysis of both *Sir Gawain and the Green Knight* and *The Battle of Maldon* to strengthen the social criticism within his fictional works. The chapter looks first at "The Tale of Turin" (which has six different published versions); it is the first tale Tolkien began to write for *The Silmarillion* and exemplifies Tolkien's social criticism at an early stage. Basically, Tolkien is mirroring Anglo-Saxon *ofermod* in the severe and over-the top actions of his dark protagonist, Turin son of Húrin. Within the tale Tolkien's social criticism is very limited: the true nature of Turin's *ofermod* is convoluted, there is no servant figure to take the place of Turin's *ofermod,* and a distinction between social æsthetic and higher morality is not given. Still, a gradation of social reflection can be distinguished between the earlier and later versions of the tale, and even with the tale's inevitable limitation, there are clear signs that Tolkien was interested in his work as social criticism; the placement of Tolkien's secondary creation in faerie does not mean that it has no social relevance. In truth, there is great social relevance even in the earliest of Tolkien's tales.

The chapter continues by examining another tale from Tolkien's *Silmarillion* and *Book of Lost Tales Part Two*, the Tale of Beren and Lúthien, which is the only major tale of Tolkien's which has romantic interest near its central theme. The telling is important, however, because it exhibits a development of social criticism and Tolkien's heroic code over Tolkien's earlier tale of Turin. Importantly, within the earlier and later versions of the tale, as with the tale of Turin, there is an observable development in Tolkien's heroic code. Also, Tolkien has integrated his interpretation of *Sir Gawain and the Green Knight,* so within the tale there is a questioning of a social æsthetic by its two true heroes, Lúthien and the faithful hound Huan, and a transgression of flawed social code for a higher moral ordering. Important as well is Tolkien's development of a heroic layering of subservient characters: Lúthien is loyal to Beren, and Huan is loyal to Lúthien, thus, to some small degree, Huan may be seen as an earlier version of Sam Gamgee.

Chapter Five concludes by analyzing Tolkien's advances in his heroic code within his child's story, *The Hobbit.* Tolkien finally gives a specific answer to *ofermod* in his creation of the Hobbit, but the narrative structure of his children's story is episodic, the monster encounters disconnected; there is not the malign will of Sauron within the story, and likewise there is a weakness of Tolkien's moral message. The dwarves and Bilbo with them (until the end of the narrative) act for the betterment of only themselves in their hope to reclaim the dwarf halls stolen by Smaug. The questing of the narrative is traditional, not the anti-quest exhibited in the *The Lord of The Rings*, and homosocial bonds are weak; Bilbo does not truly serve a lord or a lord eternal until the conclusion of the narrative when he gives his services to Bard after recognizing the *ofermod* in Thorin's actions, but even still the bond he develops is weak, as is the bond between the band of dwarves and their master Thorin. Still, *The Hobbit* is of great importance to Tolkien's social narrative because of its introduction of his secondary-created anti-hero, the Hobbit, and also because the story introduces the One Ring, a mere magic toy within *The Hobbit* but a symbol for supreme power in the *The Lord of The Rings*.

A Moral Conclusion, the concluding portion of this study, gives some broad analysis of the successes as a social critic Tolkien achieves within the *The Lord of The Rings*: the anti-quest and relinquishing of absolute power through Sam and Frodo's destruction of the Ring, Sam Gamgee as the embodiment of Tolkien's heroic code, and the deeper morality of Tolkien's created world within the text. The chapter concludes with the important recognition of the social relevance of Tolkien's world; Tolkien was operating as a social critic, his secondary-created world built upon and reflecting his primary world. He wrote against the social changes he saw occurring in the world, as he saw mechanized society given over to monsters of chaos and the rise of machines, and a gradual distancing of religious and moral truth. Ultimately, Tolkien laments a past that can never be reclaimed, his work a reflection upon the deeper moral truths and a call for the re-evaluation of technology, progress, and the heroic.

There is also an appendix to this study. Within the Appendix is included: A brief analysis of Tom Bombadil in relation to Tolkien's heroic æsthetic; a brief analysis of Tolkien's heroic women; an analysis of Tolkien's short story, *Leaf By Niggle*, which furthers the study's observations on Tolkien's religion and the moral and spiritual importance of his sub-created world; a segment from the Finnish *Kalevala* which relates to the origins of Tolkien's Tale of Turin; and, finally, a plot synopsis and analysis of the character of Fëanor from *The Silmarillion*, perhaps

Tolkien's greatest character exhibiting his interpretation of *ofermod*.

I
SOMETHING OF THE MAN

Tolkien observes in his seminal essay *The Monsters and the Critics* that *Beowulf* is "a poem from a pregnant moment in time of prose, looking back into the pit, [written] by a man learned in old tales who was struggling, as it were, to get a general view of them all" (23), specifically a man enlightened by Christ, as Tolkien considered himself to be. And like the Beowulf poet, Tolkien too was born to a time of changing social structure: specifically to the death of the Victorian ideal and the rise of the Industrial and mechanized age; Instead of looking back into the pit for inspiration, Tolkien saw impending doom in the rise of the automated society spaced further and further away from self knowledge and religious morality.

John Ronald Reuel Tolkien was the first son of Arthur Reuel Tolkien and Mabel Suffield Tolkien. Arthur was a banker and transferred to the Bank of Africa in Bloemfontein, South Africa, where Tolkien was born in 1892. Both of Tolkien's parents died while he was still young: his father in 1896 and his mother in 1904, leaving Tolkien to be raised by a monk in the Catholic church until he won a scholarship to Oxford in 1911 (Crabbe, vii, 3). The date of Tolkien's birth is important because it places him at the end of one century and the beginning of another. "I was born in 1892 and lived ... in 'the shire' in a pre-mechanical age" (Stanton, 4). Within Tolkien's writing, there is a continuous nostalgic wish to return to the green-age of his childhood. There is also the residual dread of Africa's harsh climate embodied in the cracked landscape of Mordor.

Through Tolkien's collection of *Letters*, edited by Humphrey Carpenter, great insight can be gained into Tolkien's personal feelings toward the social changes that occurred during his lifetime. There is a general social pessimism in Tolkien's writing that parallels his Anglo-Saxon counterparts' damnation of the pagan hero; in *Beowulf*, monsters were themselves dangerously anti-heroic, characteristic of the fallen hero or fallen man and in that represented the doom of society:

> This grim spirit was called Grendel,
> mighty stalker of the marches, who held
> the moors and fens; this miserable man
> lived for a time in the land of giants,
> after the Creator had condemned him
> among Cain's race – when he killed Abel
> the eternal Lord avenged that death (Liuzza, 102-108)

Tolkien too believed in the importance of the centrality of monsters within his work, but for him, at least in part, those monsters were representative of the horrors of a growing mechanized age. Wrote Tolkien, "There is tragedy and despair of all machinery laid bare. Unlike art which is content to create a new secondary world in the mind, it attempts to actualize desire and so to create power in the world; and this can not really be done with any satisfaction" (Carpenter, 87). As answer to the deadness of machinery, Tolkien advocated a return to a rural, agricultural state of existence, one reminiscent of the feudal Anglo-Saxon state he so admired. He is considered one of the earliest conservationists and environmentalists, and *The Lord of*

The Rings has been interpreted in part as an environmental text. Wrote Tolkien, "I am (obviously) much in love with plants and above all trees, and always have been; and I find human maltreatment of them as hard to bear as some find ill-treatment of animals" (Carpenter, 220). The world of nature plays an important part within Tolkien's corpus, but it is one difficult to discern in the context of the heroic; nature, for Tolkien, is often neither good nor evil but simply is, and remains something to be respected, but Tolkien's heroic code necessarily involves the respect for and proper treatment of the natural world.

During World War II Tolkien called his son Christopher a hobbit among the Urukhai and went on to name the evil spirit embodied within the war: "mechanistic, scientific, materialism, socialism of [society's] factories... at war" (110). Tolkien lost his close friend Rob Gilson during the First World War. Wrote Tolkien on the loss of his friend, "so far my chief impression is that something has gone crack... I don't feel a member of a complete body now" (10). Later, such sentiment would echo in the breakup of the fellowship of the ring. War and destruction play a central part in *The Lord of the Rings* and *The Silmarillion* and the Battle of the Five Armies occurs as the true climax within *The Hobbit*. After the death of his parents, two world wars shaped further tragedy into Tolkien's life while Tolkien's Middle-earth is shaped into a new age by war which threatens the destruction of all civilization, and brings in its conclusion the Forth Age, the Age of Man. The heroic for Tolkien would come to represent, in part, a penitent and reluctant hero who was able to bring peace in a time of chaos.

What is important within these brief biographical snippets is the insight gained into Tolkien's mindset, but more importantly they are harbingers of Tolkien's ultimate success, his social critique of an age obsessed with power, specifically power to dominate and destroy. While Tolkien still utilized characters of *ofermod* to characterize men of indomitable will within his fictional corpus, primarily in his earlier works, and less and less directly in his later, his focus turns more upon contemporary social problems, and on ways to address those problems within his fictional world. The leaders in Tolkien's world were still guilty of *ofermod*, but now the destruction that their brashness caused occurred at a global level. Tolkien removes these leaders from the centrality of his narrative to give space to his newly created hero, the Hobbit.

Ultimately, Tolkien would create a moralistic hero of subservient type (Bilbo, Frodo, Sam) and pit that reluctant character against the representatives of *ofermod* of Tolkien's age. The social code which threatened the twentieth century was the will for absolute power and illegitimate control over the earth and humanity which Tolkien saw reflected in the first two World Wars and later during the Cold War between the United States and Russia. Tolkien's major success comes when he utilizes his scholarly observations of social criticism within *The Battle of Maldon* and *Sir Gawain and the Green Knight* in context with the impending disaster of World War and atomic warfare; of course, this is set in a fantastical world of heroes and monsters, pure good versus pure evil, in a world on the verge of ultimate change. Wrote Tolkien in his *Letters,* "My fairy story must, as all art, reflect and contain in solution elements of moral and religious truth (or error) but not explicit, not in the known form of the primary 'real' world" (121). Tolkien's ultimate fruition of faerie must be seen as embodied within *The Lord of the Rings,* for within the tale Tolkien's master craft is not only a superlative sub-creation of fantasy, but it is a creation with relevant insight into the primary world and which was, in part, to be used as a model to critique the age that Tolkien knew. This is not to discredit Tolkien's other works which, though not as socially relevant, show his great endeavor for the crafting of his world, as well as his Anglo-Saxon influences, and in many cases show the development of high art in Tolkien's poetic craft and social critique.

Tolkien came upon his Hobbit quite by surprise (he wrote,

"In the ground there lived a hobbit" on a blank page of a student's school certificate paper), but with this creation Tolkien was able to effectively take the modern, or more accurately, the Victorian ideals[5] of the end of the nineteenth century, and enmesh his morals and æsthetics within that specific race of fairy creature. To posit that the Hobbit was anachronistic to Tolkien's Middle-earth would only be partially correct since Bilbo, Frodo, Sam, Pippin, Merry, and the rest of the Shire were not modern renditions of people or æsthetics from Tolkien's age; rather they represented Tolkien's sentiments towards a lost childhood and a simpler age of agricultural and rural plenitude, and they served as the moral center of Middle-earth and the newly created heroic code that Tolkien espoused. Because Tolkien gathered from multiple ideals and eras, Tolkien's Hobbit was just as anachronistic to his own age as they would have been to the heroic past of the Anglo-Saxons. At the same time, the hobbits serve as the underling figure found on the outskirts of the Old English corpus of poetry. Bilbo is, in fact, the thief who steals the goblet from the dragon's hoard:

> Three hundred winters that threat to the people
> held in the ground his great treasure,
> wondrously powerful, until one man
> made him boil with fury; he bore to his liege-lord
> the plated cup, begged for peace
> from his lord. Then the hoard was looted,
> the hoard of rings fewer, a favor was granted
> the forlorn man; for the first time
> his lord looked on that ancient work of men (Luizza 2278-2286)

Likewise, Bilbo steals a goblet from Smaug's horde to prove his worth to Thorin, King Under the Mountain, leader of the dwarves: "Above him the sleeping dragon lay, a dire menace even in his sleep. He grasped a great two-handed cup, as heavy as he could carry, and cast one fearful eye upwards. Smaug stirred a wing, opened a claw, the rumble of his snoring changed its note" (Hobbit, 214). Little is known about the thief in *Beowulf* (who actually perishes in the rage of the dragon soon after he is introduced in the poem), but it can be speculated that this minor character was picked up by Tolkien and placed at the center of his children's story,6 imbuing that character with Tolkien's heroic æsthetic and fulfilling the role of the "heroic" in place of the absent typical Anglo-Saxon warrior.

As Tolkien's modern social commentary strengthens, the hobbits of his stories take up more and more space, which culminates in book six of *The Lord of the Rings* and the casting of the Ring into Mount Doom, the ultimate sacrificial act symbolic for the refusal of unjust power. Wrote Tolkien on Sauron's Ring, "You can make the Ring into an allegory of our time, if you like; an allegory of the inevitable fate that waits for all attempts to defeat evil power by power" (Carpenter, 121). By the end of *The Lord of the Rings* Tolkien has transmuted the purpose and theme of Anglo-Saxon heroism while maintaining the form of heroic quest and strife elevated to the utmost importance by the centrality of monsters (with the dragon typifying the greatest of all threats and often placed climactically for the hero's own destruction); Tolkien continued to use his analysis of *ofermod* in *The Battle of Maldon* in his fictional texts, but is able to apply such social criticism to modernity, making his epic a moral tale for his time. Wrote Tolkien, "[*The Lord of the Rings'* center] is not in strife and war and heroism but in freedom, peace, ordinary life, and good living" (Carpenter, 105).

Bilbo and Frodo thus become vessels for Tolkien's heroism, which is a product of Tolkien's morality and æsthetic code. Their heroism can, in fact, be reduced to three main tenets which exist within Tolkien's interpretation of a moral hero, which is in actuality a medley of the Victorian æsthetic and Tolkien's devout Catholic beliefs. Although romantic love does occur occasionally in Tolkien's corpus (and even more rarely occurs as the central story theme, as is the case of the story of Beren and Lúthien found in *The Book of Lost Tales Book Two*, *The Silmarillion*, and, in brief summary, *The Children of Húrin*), for the most part romantic interest is avoided in Tolkien's heroic code. Instead,

Tolkien enforces a trinity of attributes[7] which must be accredited again to his social conditioning; those attributes would be: respect for the natural world and a life in pastoral tranquility near but not within the wilds of nature, a strong homosocial bond between the male characters (as is exemplified in the first volume of *The Lord of the Rings, The Fellowship of the Ring*), and above both of these a religious morality and providential view of the world and its inhabitants. Wrote Tolkien, "There is a place called heaven where the good here unfinished is completed; and where the stories unwritten, and the hopes unfulfilled, are continued" (Carpenter, 55). As Tolkien's social criticism develops so do these three attributes which are given over to the character of the heroic Hobbit, and strengthen the moral and religious truth in the *The Lord of The Rings*. To put Tolkien's pessimistic social views into a religious context it is again useful to look at his *Letters*:

> We were born in a dark age out of due time (for us). But there is a comfort: otherwise we should not know, or so much love, what we do love. I imagine a fish out of water is the only fish to have an inkling of water. Also we will have small swords to use. 'I will not bow before the Iron Crown, nor cast my own small golden scepter down.' Have at the Orcs, with winged words, *hildenaeddan* (war-adders), biting darts – but make sure of the mark before shooting (64).

Tolkien's sentiments are critical of his society, and provide strong support that he wished his writing to be both socially relevant and to actively address the problems he saw occurring in his time.

2

BEGINNING WITH BEORHTNOTH

The use of the Old English term *ofermod*8 in *The Battle of Maldon* has been the center of much critical debate and controversy. For his part, Tolkien interpreted the term as specifically derogatory social criticism of Beorhtnoth's prideful actions in battle which forfeited not only his life but the lives of the men beneath him. Many critics have and continue to be in disagreement with Tolkien's interpretation of *ofermod*.9 For the purpose of this study, however, only Tolkien's analysis of the word is of interest, for it is the explicit purpose of the study to identify Tolkien's scholarly critical analysis within his fictional corpus, and to provide the connection between his two fields of interest as one of social criticism. Tolkien specifically identifies the usage of the term *ofermod* as social criticism of Beorhtnoth on the part of the poet; while his critical essays identify this point, his fictional creations recreate and expand upon the earlier poem: Tolkien applies *ofermod* to his time and age.

J.R.R. Tolkien's brief play *The Homecoming of Beorhtnoth Beorhthelm's Son*, inspired by the Old English poem *The Battle of Maldon* helps illustrate Tolkien's view of the Old English word *ofermod*, which he interpreted as the excessive pride and brashness of heroes.[10] For Tolkien, the entire poem acts as a continuation of the initial social critique given by Beorhtnoth's *ofermod*.[11] Tolkien took special note of what he saw as a social critique of the Anglo-Saxon heroic code in *The Battle of Maldon* and *Beowulf*, and much of his fictional corpus worked to further critique and later gave specific answer to Old English *ofermod*. What is critical to Tolkien's approach, however, is that he did not leave *ofermod* in the Anglo-Saxon past, but endeavored to show how *ofermod* might be applied to the modern social situation.[12]

In *Homecoming* two servants of Beorhtnoth, the son of Beorhthelm, the duke of Essex, come to collect Beorhtnoth's body which has been hacked to death by Northmen who, led by Anlaf, invaded England in 991 during the reign of Æthelred II (TR, 3). What is exceptional about the battle, and the cause for England's loss, is Beorhtnoth's allowance of the Vikings to cross a ford unharmed to permit a fair battle. Both Tolkien's rendition of the event and the Old English poem itself serve as examples of a larger social problem within Anglo-Saxon England, specifically the heroic leader's immediacy in battle, and the importance of his heroism or adherence to a heroic code above his safety and the safety of his people. The Anglo-Saxon leader held the welfare of his people in his corporeal self, his death possibly leading to the death of his nation, as is foreshadowed at the end of the *Beowulf* poem. Tolkien understood *ofermod* as a social critique by *The Battle of Maldon* poet and applied *ofermod* to his own work,[13] not only to retain the flavor of the world painted within the Anglo-Saxon poems, but to eventually cultivate a more original method to critique the problematic social changes he perceived occurring during his own life.

What is most important about Tolkien's *The Homecoming of Beorhtnoth Beorhthelm's Son* is that its purpose is easily recognizable as a basic critique of Anglo-Saxon heroism and *ofermod*, and thus serves as a clear starting point for Tolkien's development of his own heroism and heroic attributes. In the vein of *The Battle of Maldon* poet, Tolkien gives a critique of a social structure.[14] Like the poem, Tolkien has yet to provide a specific answer to the social problem (which he later does in his superlative work *The Lord of the Rings*), and does not yet use his observations on *ofermod* to critique his own social conditions (Rather, in his short play, he is only mirroring how he interprets the word *ofermod* and its social implications within the poem.)

Similar to the Old English poet of *The Battle of Maldon*, Tolkien uses the voice of the subordinate within Anglo-Saxon society to critique the "chivalric" role of the heroic leader. In *Homecoming*, the voice of critical observation is given over entirely to its two actors, Torhthelm and Tidwald, while their liege Beorhtnoth is silenced in death. Their conversation echoes in part the words of Beorhtwold, Beorhtnoth's man from the Old English poem:

> Our hearts must grow resolute, our courage more valiant,
> our spirits must be greater, though our strength grows less.
> Here lies our Lord all hewn down,
> goodly he lies in the dust. A kinsman mourns
> that who now from this battle-play thinks to turn away.
> I am advanced in years. I do not desire to be taken away,
> but I by my liege Lord,
> by that favorite of men I intend to lie. (312-319)

Tolkien's Torhthelm and Tidwald recognize that they, like Beorhtwold, are dependent upon the good fortune of their lord, but Tidwald's speech is also filled with sardonic sarcasm over their situation with little feeling of loss for his dead lord. He is a somewhat enlightened servant who holds within his conversation Tolkien's insight into the Anglo-Saxon social structure. Tidwald does not pity his dead lord so much, for he understands that Beorhtnoth's brash actions are at fault and that Beorhtnoth acted wrongfully. Says Tidwald to Torhthelm,

> No more's the pity.
> Alas, my friend, our lord was at fault,
> or so in Maldon this morning men are saying.

> Too proud, too princely! But his pride's
> > Cheated,
> And his princedom has passed, so we'll praise
> > His valor.
> He let them cross the causeway, so keen was he
> To give minstrels matter for mighty songs.
> Needlessly noble. It should not have been:
> Bidding bows be still, and the bridge opening,
> Matching more with few and in mad hand-strokes!
> Well, doom he dared, and died for it (TR, 16)

Tidwald acts as the voice of criticism within the work. He recognizes Beorhnoth's *ofermod* and pokes jibes at his dead lord which no true Anglo-Saxon servant would ever dare: "Beorhtnoth we bare not Beowulf here: / no pyres for him, nor piling of mounds; / and the gold will be given to the good abbot" (12) and "By Edmund's head! Though his is now missing, our Lord's not light" (16), but Tidwald's glib remarks are more than just comical sidelines for the reader. He makes an important distinction between Beowulf and Beorhnoth for (as Tolkien relates in his commentary following the play) Beowulf acted as a subordinate to Hygelac, lord of the Geats, and his bodily intervention against Grendel and Grendel's mother in Heorot does not put the nation of the Geats directly in danger, for Hygelac is ensconced safely back at home on his throne, ensuring the safety of his people (TR 22-23). It is only in the second half of the poem, when Beowulf has become king, and gives himself to bodily harm and ultimately death fighting the firedrake that his actions truly mirror Beorhtnoth's *ofermod*.

Anglo-Saxon heroism is dead in Tolkien's play, literally, and the space of the work is given over to the subordinates who are left in a world without a leader; it is a dying world (due in no small part to *ofermod*), but Tolkien gives some hope. While Torhthelm's pessimism mirrors Beorhtwold, Tidwald is more resolute and he is not yet ready to give his life over to woe because of the destruction of his lord and dissolution of his welfare. Says Tidwald, "I have cares of my own / in my heart, Totta, and my head's weary. / I am sorry for you, and for myself also. / Sleep, lad, then! Sleep! The slain won't trouble, / if your head be heavy, or the wheels grumble... / There's food ahead and fair stables" (TR, 18). Tidwald shows no remorse for his dead lord. He is very literally Tolkien's voice of criticism, while Torhthelm's voice remains one of social pessimism and resignation and his ending remarks reflect upon the state of England's social decay during the reign of Æthelred:

> There are candles in the dark and cold voices.
> I hear mass chanted for master's soul
> In Ely isle. Thus ages pass,
> And men after men. Mourning voices
> Of women weeping. So the world passes;
> Day follows day, and dust gathers,
> His tomb crumbles, as time gnaws it,
> And his kith and kindred out of ken dwindle.
> So men flicker and in the mirk go out.
> The world withers and the wind rises;
> The candles are quenched. Cold falls the night.
> It's dark! It's dark, and doom coming! (TR, 19)

Torhthelm is unable to distinguish a flawed social ideology from a higher moral truth. He confuses social ills with a moral doom, thus his fears are intensified and he is not able to enact change to his situation.

The enlightened Tidwald is more resolute, and though he recognizes that "The roads are rough and rest is short/ for English men in Æthelred's day" (20), he, like Tolkien, is aware that it is only because of a social imposition upon the people, not some greater moral doom, and that the trouble will perhaps pass with social change and renewal; Tidwald, as Tolkien's mouthpiece, is able to distinguish the social ideology from a higher moral structure. Says Tidwald to Torhthelm, "Aye, a bump on the bone is bad for dreams, / and it's cold waking. But your words are queer... / with your talk of wind / and doom and a dark ending... / When morning comes, it'll be much like others" (TR 19-20).

What Tolkien has begun to do in *The Homecoming* is to take

Anglo-Saxon heroism and place it at the border of his creative work. Not only does he begin to critique the social code of heroism but he raises the subordinate, the Wiglaf and the Beorhtwold, and places their struggle at the center of his work. He is more interested in the endeavors of the faithful servant than the heroic leader, so that the heroic leaders within Tolkien's work are in truth the faithful servants, or the servants of the faithful servants, as is the case with Samwise Gamgee to Frodo Baggins. Tolkien gradually changes the Anglo-Saxon heroic code (as he interprets it through *ofermod*) to bring focus upon the outskirts and the blind-faith of the servant.[15] Here it is important to remember the dual meaning of lord in the Old English language, for Tolkien is referring also to the second meaning, the heavenly lord, and the servant's fidelity to religious faith.[16]

Tolkien's endeavor to place the servant in the center of his narrative and the traditional heroic leader at the borders can be observed through the course of Tolkien's writings.[17] While Tolkien's earlier works are more replicate of his interpretation of *ofermod* in *The Battle of Maldon*, his later works (*The Hobbit* and *The The Lord of The Rings*) center around hobbits and show movement away from a mere replication or criticism of *ofermod*. The hobbits themselves deserve special consideration for the part they play in Tolkien's reconstruction of heroism, both as a critique of Anglo-Saxon heroism, but also as a model for the modern reader, and those attributes of life which Tolkien saw as intrinsic to good living. It is interesting to note as well that Tolkien's popular success comes with his creation of the Hobbit figure, and with what shall be shown as a growing social code which utilized Tolkien's interpretation of *ofermod* as well as his interpretations of a moral ordering to *Sir Gawain and the Green Knight* (to be discussed later).

Tolkien's ultimate purpose was one of a philologist endeavoring to create a world in which his created languages would exist naturally (specifically it began with the elven phrase, *"Elen si la lumen omentielvo,"* translated: "a star shines on the hour of our meeting"), but one can not ignore Tolkien's personal experiences and moral judgment at the heroic center of the Middle-earth he created. Some foreshadowing of Tolkien's heroism comes in Tolkien's commentary following *The Homecoming* which begins the collection of his work found within the *Tolkien Reader*:

> [The servants'] part was to endure and die, and not to question, though a recording poet may fairly comment that someone had blundered. In their situation heroism was superb. Their duty was unimpaired by the error of their master, and (more importantly) neither in the hearts of those near to the old man was love lessened. It is the heroism of the obedience and love not of pride or willfulness that is the most heroic and the most moving, from Wiglaf under his kinsman's shield, to Beorhtwold at Maldon (TR, 25).

Tolkien's sentiments show his interest in the servant figure. He would work to bring the servant figure from the outskirts of Anglo-Saxon texts such as *Beowulf* to the center of his own narrative. His Hobbit, imbued with Tolkien's heroic æsthetic, would represent a new type of hero and social model meant to counteract the *ofermod* Tolkien saw occurring in his own time.

3

TOLKIEN'S HEROIC AESTHETIC

In "Taking the Part of Trees: Eco-Conflict in Middle-earth," Verlyn Flieger begins to address the complicated matter of nature within Tolkien's Middle-earth. Flieger notes that Tolkien was considered "as a kind of advanced man for the Green Movement" and that in the fictional characters of Tom Bombadil, Goldberry, Old Man Willow, Ghanburi-ghan, and Treebeard Tolkien gives a voice to the natural world (147). Tolkien takes the part of trees and nature; his fairy world is populated by as many fictional species of tree as humanoid: "Laurelin, Teleperion, the White Tree, the Party Tree, the mallorns of Lothlórien, Niggle's Tree, Finglas, Fladrif, Fimbrethil, Bregalad... and even the avenging Huorns" (147). Even in Tolkien's early mythology and founding of Middle-earth in *The Silmarillion* nature is central:

> And it is said by the Eldar that in water there lives yet the echo of the Music of the Ainur (elves) more than in any substance else that is in this Earth; and many of the Children of Ilúvatar (Ainur) hearken still unsated to the voices of the Sea, and yet know not for what they listen (19).

Tolkien even gives the source of original light in his sub-created world (after the two pillars of light have been destroyed by Melko) to two beautiful trees which the goddess Yavanna sings into creation. The fruit of these two trees would later become the sun and the moon:

> In seven hours the glory of each tree waxed full and waned again to naught; and each awoke once more to life an hour before the other ceased to shine. Thus in Valinor twice every day there came a gentle hour of soft light when both trees were faint and their gold and silver beams were mingled (38).

Tolkien's vision of nature was not so simplistic, however, to limit nature imagery to just the "good" aspects of his creation, for trees and nature imagery nearly as often signify strife and growing doom, such as is the case with Mirkwood in *The Hobbit* and the Old Forest in *The Lord of The Rings*. Just as often mountains are Tolkien's symbol of choice when depicting the opposition of good, such as Mount Doom. Tolkien's greatest villain of all, Melko, the fallen Ainur or Holy One to whom Sauron is but a servant, took on the shape of a great mountain:

> [Melko's] envy grew then the greater within him; and he also took visible form, but because of his mood and the malice that burned in him that form was dark and terrible. And he descended upon Arda in power and majesty greater than any other of the Valar, as a mountain that wades in the sea and has its head above the clouds and is clad in ice and crowned with smoke and fire; and the light of the eyes of Melkor was like a flame that withers with heat and pierces with a deadly cold (*Silmarillion*, 22).

There is a duality of purpose within Tolkien's nature æsthetic. His first usage of nature relates back to Tolkien's Victorian ideals and his early childhood. The nostalgia within Tolkien's writing hopes to regain the green-wood and the pastoral tranquility of an agrarian culture, which is best exemplified in the hobbits' Shire. Nature depicted within the Shire is, however, a very different type than the one Tolkien's heroic adventurers encounter on the quest. The Shire is, in fact, a locus of controlled or tamed nature which provides respite for Tolkien's heroes during the interludes of monster encounter. The Shire, like Heorot (after Grendel has been expelled), is representative of a social center. Similar centers of tamed nature include Elrond's Last Homely Home and Beorn's home in *The Hobbit:*

> [Beorn] lives in an oak-wood and has a great wooden house; and as a man he keeps cattle and horses which are nearly as marvelous as himself. They work for him and talk to him... He keeps hives and hives of great fierce bees, and lives most on cream and honey. As a bear he ranges far and wide (Hobbit, 115).

In Tolkien's *Fellowship of the Ring* these naturalistic loci of rest are represented first in Tom Bombadil and Goldberry's home, again in Elrond's Last Homely Home, and finally Galadriel's Lothlórien wood:

> They went along many paths and climbed many stairs, until they came to the high places and saw before them amid a wide lawn a fountain shimmering. It was lit by silver lamps that swung from the boughs of trees, and it fell into a basin of silver, from which a white stream spilled. Upon the south side of the lawn there stood the mightiest of all the trees; its great smooth bole gleamed like grey silk, and upon it towered, until its first branches, far above, opened their huge limbs under shadowy clouds of leaves (FR, 458).

Tolkien has gathered such places of rest and regeneration from multiple epic traditions.[18] Loci of rest are an integral part of the heroic quest which Tolkien utilized as part of the primary action of his stories, but when analyzed in context of Tolkien's growing modern social criticism, these places of peaceful nature come to represent something beyond the literary patterning of an epic quest. Flieger recognizes in part Tolkien's attempt at social criticism of the mechanized age, but he comes too quickly to the conclusion that Tolkien accepted an inevitable conflict between man and nature. Flieger stipulates that what Tolkien depicts within his fictional corpus is but a natural state of strife which man creates as he attempts to fortify himself against life's perils. Writes Flieger, "If we live and work and eat and build, even if we plant and prune and tend and cherish, it is inevitable that we alter nature, and in that alteration it is also inevitable that some of the things we would wish to preserve will be irretrievably lost" (157). Such an assumption falls short of Tolkien's heroic æsthetic, for he is certainly making distinctions in his work on how different civilizations of races interact with their environment. Remember the purpose of his sub-creation was to reflect on the primary world, and in this context Tolkien's races and their relationship with nature must serve as a social model which Tolkien hopes his reader will observe and take lesson from.

To understand Tolkien's nature æsthetic pertaining to the modern age, one must return to his major concern of a society devoid of nature: a non-living, iron place, ruled by a domineering will. While Tolkien's representation of nature does serve, in part, as a perilous realm in which his heroes' strengths are put to the test, when nature is depicted in association with humanity it always reflects upon the social codes which govern that society. Tolkien's depictions of nature in relation to society are a byproduct of his larger social concern exemplified in the Ring, a will towards absolute power, an overreaching power restricted to a realm beyond man's moral grasp.[19] Societies of this type, led by the false leaders who exhibit *ofermod* and hope to wield absolute power, use nature, and man, as pure commodities in a blind and reckless attempt to obtain materialistic wealth and power. Saruman's actions in Orthanc exemplify this well. Fangorn speaks of this in *The Two Towers*:

> [Saruman] and his foul folk are making havoc now. Down on the borders they are felling trees – good trees... hewn up and carried off to feed the fires of Orthanc... Many of those trees were my friends, creatures I had known from nut and acorn; many had voices of their own that are lost forever now (TT 91).

In both *The Hobbit* and *The Lord of The Rings*, Tolkien's dwarves' greedy quest for wealth and overuse of natural resources are also a representation of the type of society Tolkien is criticizing. In *The Hobbit* the dwarfish horde draws the attention of the greedy dragon, Smaug, while in *The Fellowship* the result of the dwarves' greed is exemplified in the Balrog and goblin infestation of Moria. Speaks Gimli during the *Council of Elrond*:

> 'Moria! Moria! Wonder of the Northern world! Too deep we delved there, and woke the nameless fear. Long have its vast mansions lain empty since the children of Durin fled. But now we spoke of it again with longing, and yet with dread; for no dwarf has dared to pass the doors of Khazad-dum for many lives of kings, save Thror alone, and he perished' (316).

Nature without society, for Tolkien, is a realm dangerous and powerful, one which is beyond his moralistic battle of good and evil. An evil society may, in part, corrupt and destroy nature, and even Tolkien's idyllic Shire upsets the woods surrounding it by expanding its borders too far. For Tolkien, the natural balance of the world is upset through a corrupted, amoral society. It is worthwhile to note here that when nature rises up or grows evil, it acts in Tolkien's world in a similar way to his monsters: both as a challenge for his heroes, but also as a critique of the unnaturalness of the modernized society in servitude to the machine. Nature personified acts for Tolkien in a similar way as Grendel's invasion of Heorot in the *Beowulf* poem, as a punishment for an immoral society:

> Thus the foe of mankind, fearsome and solitary,
> often committed his many crimes,
> cruel humiliations; he occupied Heorot,
> the jewel-adorned hall, in the dark of nights –
> he saw no need to salute the throne...
> At times they offered honor to idols
> At pagan temples, prayed aloud
> That the soul-slayer might offer assistance
> In the country's distress. Such was their custom,
> The hope of heathens (Luizza, 164- 67, 175-79)

Here the *Beowulf* poet implies that Grendel serves as a plague sent from a true god to punish heathens. Although Tolkien's use of nature within his social criticism is not explicitly a reflection of religious immorality of his age, nature nevertheless serves to critique those elements in society which Tolkien saw as corruptive, specifically the mechanization of society and the overwhelming power which dangerously wielded new and volatile technology. (And it is certain that he must have seen a distancing of the mechanized society from religion as a major concern.)

Tolkien's nature is in part first representative of the Victorian Age and a wish to return to a simpler time, and, second, it serves Tolkien's social critique, for nature in turmoil is emblematic of a society in turmoil, and the byproduct of unjustified and unchecked striving for a power to dominate. Tolkien lamented on his lost world, "The heart has gone out of the little kingdom, and the woods and plains are aerodromes and bomb-practice targets... Machines are becoming the privileged class, the machines are going to be enormously more powerful" (Carpenter, 113). Tolkien's hero then must both befriend nature and save nature from an unnatural destruction (just as Pippin and Merry befriend Fangorn and, with the ents, destroy Orthanc), but at the same time Tolkien's heroes must remain wary of the natural force embodied in nature. Sam is a clear example of such a hero, for not only does he aid Frodo in defeating Sauron, but he is also given magical seeds and earth from Galadriel and uses them to revive the Shire after Sauron and Wormtongue have scoured it. The destroyed Shire serves as a warning and as a mirror for what Tolkien sees as happening to the natural world in his own time, while Sam's conservationist actions serve as social model:

> As they crossed the bridge and looked up the Hill they gasped. Even Sam's vision in the Mirror had not prepared him for what they saw. The Old Grange on the west side had been knocked down, and its place taken by rows of tarred sheds. All the chestnuts were gone. The banks and hedgerows were broken. Great wagons were standing in disorder in a field beaten bare of grass. Bagshot Row was a yawning sand and gravel quarry. Bag End up beyond could not be seen for a

clutter of large huts.
'They've cut it down!' cried Sam. 'They've cut down the Party Tree!' (RK, 366)

Through Sam's heroic actions, however, the Shire is restored to an even more splendid natural beauty than it had before the scouring:

> Spring surpassed his wildest hopes. His trees began to sprout and grow, as if time was in a hurry and wished to make one year do for twenty. In the Party Field, a beautiful young sapling leaped up: it had silver bark and long leaves and burst into golden flowers in April. It was indeed a *mallorn,* and it was the wonder of the neighbourhood. In after years, as it grew in grace and beauty, it was known far and wide and people would come long journeys to see it: the only *mallorn* west of the Mountains and east of the Sea, and one of the finest in the world (RK, 375).

Sam then is a character imbued with Tolkien's heroic æsthetic of a respect for the natural world, and serves as a model of action for modern society.[20]

As an Oxford don Tolkien was a member of a group of likeminded writers and academics who called themselves the Inklings. Tolkien's close friend C.S. Lewis was part of this group and together with other male friends, Tolkien and Lewis would share their work while enjoying a round of beers at the local pub. Writes Brenda Partridge in her essay, "No Sex Please – We're Hobbits: The Construction of the Female Sexuality in The Lord of the Rings": "The group met frequently and regularly to discuss their own writing and other literary and academic matters. Characteristically of the British male of a particular socio-economic class, marked forever by school life in an exclusively male school (often boarding school), the group tried to carry into adult life the club clannishness it members had enjoyed at school" (179). Tolkien remained a product of his time and education and although there is every reason to believe that he loved his wife, Edith Bratt, he shared strong homosocial bonds with his fellow academics, and this social æsthetic carried over to his creative works.

Within the close knit group of educated friends there was a general snobbery towards and disapproval of the female element. Wrote Lewis in his diary in 1922, "A friend dead is to be mourned, a friend married is to be guarded against, both equally lost" (Inklings 162). Tolkien shared an "equally dismissive view of female intellect," though it should be said that in his writing there are many exquisitely developed female heroines who function along the perimeter of his male-driven heroism. However, in 1941 Tolkien wrote:

> How quickly an intelligent woman can be taught, grasp the teacher's ideas, see his point – and how (with some exceptions) they can go no further, when they leave his hand, or when they cease to take a personal interest in him. It is their gift to be receptive, stimulated, fertilized (in many other matters than the physical) by the male (Inklings, 169).

Within the Inklings, Tolkien and Lewis shared an even closer relationship. Partridge speculates that there might have been an "erotic element" to the two men's relationship, though she is careful to remain speculative about this assumption, and later properly concludes that "it would not be sensible to push this evidence any further" (182). Writes Partridge, "An understanding of Lewis's ambiguous sexuality and latent sadism gives dimension to the seemingly chance remark about Tolkien soon after they first met. Lewis described him as 'a smooth, pale, fluent, little chap... thinks all literature is written for the amusement of men between thirty and forty... No harm in him: only needs a smack or so'" (182). As Tolkien and Lewis's relationship grew, though, Tolkien and his wife began sleeping in separate beds, and when Tolkien and Lewis's relationship became strained and a gradual separation between the two occurred after Lewis befriended Charles Williams, Tolkien wrote: "We were separated first by the sudden apparition of Charles Williams, and then by his marriage. But we owed a great debt to the other, and that tie, with the deep affection that it begot, remained" (Inklings, 252). It is even speculated that Tolkien represented this intense homosocial triangle within *The Lord of The Rings* with Williams depicted through Gollum, Lewis through Frodo, and Tolkien himself through Sam.

What becomes manifest within Tolkien's work are these strong bonds of male friendship, a social æsthetic Tolkien took from his own life and placed into the sub-creation of Middle-earth. Tolkien's heroes, especially his two strongest, Sam and Frodo, share a bond with one another which grows through the course of their travels; it is a bond of platonic love and respect for similarities in tastes and virtues, and though Tolkien's heroes are affectionate to one another it is important to distinguish their actions from any erotic or homosexual urges, simply because it is not very likely that there are any. Tolkien's homosocial æsthetic echoed the Victorian Age of male intellectual superiority; it was also the world he was brought up in, and a part of himself he did not question. Tolkien's field of study, the Anglo-Saxon poems, were also strongly centered upon male relationships, specifically lord-servant relationships, so it was only natural that Tolkien utilize that aspect of his study in the development of his heroic creation. This might, however, be seen as a weak point in Tolkien's writing, for it seems that he did not reconsider his society's views towards women, but accepted them almost as natural and religious truth; so, regarding women's role in society, Tolkien is a rather poor social critic.

In the homosocial realm of Tolkien's world, the hobbits may in fact embody the "club clannishness" Tolkien never questioned or grew out of. Reflects Edwin Muir from *The Inklings:* "... all the characters are boys masquerading as adult heroes. The hobbits... are ordinary boys, the fully human heroes have reached the fifth form; but hardly one of them knows anything about women, except by hearsay. Even the elves and dwarves and the ents are boys irretrievably, and will never come to puberty" (223). Such observations, if true, may relate not only to Tolkien's entanglement in societies of men, but also back to the origins of *The Hobbit* as a child's fairy-tale; it would only be natural to create a childlike hero who the reader of the juvenile epic could relate to. Writes Partridge,

> Size and lack of magical power are two reasons provided to account for this care and protection of the hobbits, a third is the feudalistic basis of the relationships. Echoing the feudal society of the ancient Norse myths and the medieval tales of chivalry, the hobbits, like the rest of the warriors, play the role of vassal to the various kings. Pippin swears an oath of fealty to Denethor and, despite Denethor's madness, serves him loyally, saving Faramir from the funeral pyre lit mistakenly by Denethor in the depths of despair. Merry, too, swears allegiance to Théoden (183).

What Partridge recognizes then are the two natural sources for Tolkien's strong male relationships, the æsthetic of male bonding of his time and the æsthetic of male bonding from an age long past.[21] This again relates to Tolkien's admiration of the servant figure of the Old English tradition and the undying and unquestioning fidelity the servant showed to his lord. Such a connection comes naturally from Tolkien's endeavors to in part recreate the Anglo-Saxon secondary-created world of heroic men battling monsters, but even here Tolkien moves forward from his Anglo-Saxon counterparts, for though Merry and Pippin's relationships are ones of fealty to their lord, Tolkien's greater heroes, Sam and Frodo, show a mutual bond between servant and master.

Samwise Gamgee is the character of perfect devotion to his master, Frodo Baggins, and the relationship between Sam and Frodo is exemplary of Tolkien's homosocial æsthetic. Through the course of events, Frodo comes to owe his life to Sam when he first saves Frodo from destruction by the last remaining spawn of Ungoliant, the giant she-spider Shelob:

> Then [Sam] charged. No onslaught more fierce was ever seen in the savage world of beasts, where some desperate small creature armed with little teeth, alone, will spring upon a tower of horn and hide that stands above its fallen mate (TT, 428).

Later, Sam, wearing the One Ring, saves Frodo from the orcs, Shagrat and Gorbag, and it is Sam who carries Frodo up the crags of Mount Doom when Frodo has lost the strength to move further. While Sam wears the ring (around his neck and not on his finger), he is seemingly transformed into a great elven warrior who frightens away the orcs, but Sam's form in this altered state should also be seen as a reflection of his inner strength. Sam, given over to the power of the ring, is able to distinguish the ring's power to corrupt while Frodo succumbs to the power (and in this aspect Sam is the stronger character), mistaking Sam for a nasty orc trying to cheat him out of the Ring:

> 'I can hardly believe it,' said Frodo, clutching him. 'There was an orc with a whip, and then it turns into Sam! Then I wasn't dreaming after all when I heard that singing down below, and I tried to answer? Was it you?'
> 'It was indeed, Mr. Frodo. I'd given up hope, almost. I couldn't find you.'
> 'Well, you have now, Sam, dear Sam,' said Frodo, and he lay back in Sam's gentle arms, closing his eyes, like a child at rest when night-fears are driven away by some loved voice or hand (RK, 228).

And it is Sam who is able to reflect observationally on the actions of the story. Like Tidwald in Tolkien's *Homecoming* play, Sam is given a special insight of the author's which places his character close to Tolkien's æsthetics and ideals:

> I wonder what tale we've fallen into... Beren now, he never thought he was going to get that Silmaril from the Iron Crown in Thangorodim, and yet he did, and that was a worse place and a blacker danger than ours. But that's a long tale, of course, and goes on past the happiness and into grief and beyond it – and the Silmaril went on and came to Eärendil. And why, sir, I never thought of that before! We've got – You've got some of the light of it in that star-glass that the Lady gave you! Why, to think of it, we're in the same tale still! It's going on. Don't the great tales never end? (TT, 408)

Not only is Sam given special insight here, but through him Tolkien is utilizing the layering device of the Anglo-Saxon poets, for just as the *Beowulf* poet refers to myths of his day such as the dragon-slaying Sigemund to give Beowulf praise in comparison, so does Tolkien refer back to his great early myths of Middle-earth, *The Silmarillion*, to create depth within his narrative.

Sam is given more and more centrality in Tolkien's story as it progresses, and this shows Tolkien's wish to take the servant figure of *Beowulf* and *The Battle of Maldon* and place the heroism of such characters at the center of the narrative, giving focus to their heroism above the *ofermod* of their masters. His heroism resembles that of Wiglaf[22] who goes to the aid of Beowulf at the end of that poem, but Sam is given greater centrality to the narrative than Wiglaf, showing again Tolkien's emphasis of the heroism of the servant figure, and his rearrangement of the heroic æsthetic which took the servant figure from the perimeter of the story and placed it in the central narrative. Sam, in part, like Bilbo before him, is created from the Anglo-Saxon servant figure taken from the perimeter of poems like *Beowulf*, and given centrality in the story. Wiglaf, a pivotal character in *Beowulf*, does not appear until the concluding acts of the Anglo-Saxon poem:

> He was called Wiglaf, Weohstan's son,
> A worthy shield-warrior, a prince of the Scylfings,
> Kinsman of Aelfhere. He saw his liege-lord
> Suffer heat under his war-helmet;
> He recalled the honors he had received from him,
> The wealthy homestead of the Waegmundings,
> Every folk-right that his father had possessed;
> He could not hold back – his hand seized
> The pale linden shield, and he drew his old sword (Liuzza, 2602-2610)

What needs to be remembered and recognized here is the context in which these heroics of Sam's arise; Sam is acting out of his platonic love for Frodo, and through the events of the narrative, Sam and Frodo are gradually separated from a larger group of males; they must necessarily depend upon each other to survive in Sauron's corrupted Mordor. Not only is their bond explicitly one of a lord-servant type, but even more than this, it is one of mutual friendship and respect. Only later does Gollum arrive to trouble and harass the two. Sam and Frodo's separation from a larger male group is representative of Tolkien and Lewis's closer relationship within a larger group of male friends, the Inklings, while Gollum's pestering may reflect upon the arrival of Williams.[23]

Tolkien had higher purposes for his creative realm than simply a place for the entertainment and escape of the reader, or even a focus on social criticism (though this remains an important part of Tolkien's work and all writing); he was, in fact, actively striving to honor a Christian god, for in the act of his subcreation of a secondary world, he saw himself as mirroring a Primary creator, and honoring that creator in the process and secondary-creation of his art. Tolkien argued "that the mythological imagination could deal in a profoundly revolutionary way with serious and moral and spiritual issues" and that "living mythology can deepen rather than cloud over visions of reality" (Helms, 2), but he was careful to keep explicitly doctrinal views of religion out of his creative vision. Not only did he believe that Primary belief systems had no place in the fairy-tale realm, he also did not want his secondary-creation to be a mere allegory of biblical sermon, thus Tolkien's Middle-earth is necessarily not explicitly religious but underlining the actions of the heroes is a Divine Providence (Ilúvatar's, the Creator's, plan).

Gandalf, as a disguised Maiar (similar to a demigod), servant to the Valar (Tolkien's gods), is privy to the divine plans within Tolkien's world and warns Frodo not to behave rashly against Gollum. Later, at the story's climax, it is Gollum who bites off Frodo's finger and the Ring after Frodo's will has failed to complete his task of destroying the Ring; so it is Gollum who ultimately destroys Sauron, upholding Aragorn's remark "Oft evil will shall evil mar". After the Ring is gone, Frodo remarks to Sam, "But do you remember Gandalf's words: *Even Gollum may have something yet to do?* But for him, Sam, I could not have destroyed the Ring. The Quest would have been in vain, even at the bitter end. So let us forgive him! For the Quest is achieved, and now all is over" (RK, 277). In this context, Gandalf works as a moral guide to Tolkien's heroic hobbits who follow Gandalf almost blindly, as they would a religious leader; it is not the part of Tolkien's hero to be enlightened to the mechanics of the ordering of Middle-earth; in-fact, a character is more heroic the less he questions the nature of his world, instead serving diligently and unquestioningly those he sees as privy to a greater understanding of a divine plan (as does Sam).

Gandalf, after his resurrection from the Battle of the Peak, is privy to the divine ordering of Ilúvatar and foreshadows the doom of Sauron when he confronts the Black Captain of the Nazgul, the King of Angmen, at the destroyed gate of Gondor. Warns Gandalf, "You cannot enter here – Go back to the abyss prepared for you! Fall into the nothingness that awaits you and your master!" (125). At the end of *The Hobbit,* Gandalf reveals his awareness of a greater plan of creation in his closing remarks to Bilbo: "You don't really suppose, do you, that all your adventures and escapes were managed by mere luck, just for your sole benefit? You are a very fine person, Mr. Baggins, and I am very fond of you, but you are quite a little fellow in a wide world after all!" (303). Gandalf, however, is not the true focus of the narrative; he serves partly as a father figure to Tolkien's heroes, and partly as a religious guide to keep Tolkien's heroes from going astray.

Like Christ, Gandalf sacrifices himself for a higher purpose on the Bridge of Khaza Dum: he is resurrected and born anew as Gandalf the White early on in *The Two Towers.* Commands Gandalf on the bridge before the Balrog, "You can not pass. I am a servant of the secret fire, wielder of the flame of Anor. You cannot pass. The dark fire will not avail you, flame of Udun. Go back to the shadow! You cannot pass" (322), but in the ensuing confrontation, Gandalf is caught by the Balrog's whip and taken down to the depths and mistaken as lost by his companions. In *The Two Towers,* Gandalf returns but he has changed; he has become more powerful, for he has been granted Saruman's powers by Manwë, chief of the Valar, who has deemed Saruman unworthy. Gandalf recounts his ordeal with the Balrog to Aragorn, Legolas, and Gimli:

> We fought far under the living earth, where time is not counted. Ever he clutched me, and ever I hewed him, till at last he fled into dark tunnels. They were not made by Durin's folk, Gimli son of Gloin. Far, far below the deepest delvings of the Dwarves, the world is gnawed by nameless things. Even Sauron knows them not. They are older than he. Now I have walked there, but I will bring no report to darken the light of day. In that despair my enemy was my only hope, and I pursued him, clutching at his heel. Thus he brought me back at last to the secret ways of Khazad-dum: too well he knew them all. Ever up now we went, until we came to the Endless Stair. (134)

Gandalf continues his retelling of the epic battle, which both the reader and the other members of the fellowship are only privy to secondhand through Gandalf, and can only speculate on the "nameless things" which Gandalf mentions, but it seems obvious that Gandalf's battle has taken him beyond the mortal realm; he has become an Odinic figure, god-like, like Thor doing battle with the encircling *wyrm* at the end time of Ragnarok.

Gandalf recounts how he fought until reaching the mountain summit of Celebdil and there defeated the Balrog, but was himself destroyed, yet granted the gift of resurrection, though he does not reveal this so explicitly: 'Then darkness took me, and I stayed out of thought and time, and I wandered far on roads that I will not tell. / Naked I was sent back – for a brief time, until my task was done" (TT, 135). It is likely that Gandalf was sent to Mandros, the hall of the dead, which is placed in the farthest west of Middle-earth (even beyond the mountains of Aman, where the Valar reside). Mandros is kept by Namo, the summoner of the spirit of the slain; but through Manwë, Gandalf is allowed to return to complete the preordained design of Sauron's defeat.

In the context of Tolkien's structural form and method, Gandalf's resurrection is the greatest in a series of *eucatastrophes*, or happy endings, which Tolkien saw as necessary to the fantasy story. Wrote Tolkien on his essay, *On Fairy Stories*, "The *eucatastrophic* tale is the true form of fairy-tale, and its highest function" (TR, 85). Tolkien goes on to make an important connection between this integral element of his fictional world and what he saw as religious truth:

> I would venture to say that approaching the Christian Story from this direction, it has long been my feeling (a joyous feeling) that God redeemed the corrupt making creatures, men, in a way fitting to this aspect, as to others, of their strange nature. The Gospels contain a fairy-story, or a story of a larger kind which embraces all the essence of fairy-stories. They contain many marvels – peculiarly artistic, beautiful, and moving: 'mythical' in their perfect, self-contained significance; and among the marvels is the greatest and most complete conceivable eucatastrophe. But this story has entered History and the primary world; the desire and aspiration of subcreation has been raised to fulfillment of Creation. The Birth of Christ is the eucatastrophe of Man's history. The Resurrection is the eucatastrophe of the story of the Incarnation (TR, 89).

Tolkien saw his artistic endeavors participating in an honoring of a larger creation, and in his creative method's passive nature and refusal to manipulate the Progenitor's master design, an acceptance of Divine Will. He saw materialistic endeavors to create in conflict with the Primary motivator and not true creation, rather a manipulation and corruption of a Primary Creation. Though Tolkien's religious justification and purpose behind his work is not directly reflective of his heroic code or social commentary, religion is a necessary and all-encompassing function of Tolkien's creativity and provides the direction and underlying critical observations for Tolkien's heroic and social criticism. A religious morality functions to strengthen Tolkien's other ideals within his social criticism. Tolkien's religious morality is his meta-ideal, for it was Tolkien's foundation for how he approached life and art. His two other major ideals, that of nature and that of the homosocial code, sprang forth from Tolkien's religion. Religion is not Tolkien's explicit focus, but is the form which governs the morals of his sub-creation, just as he saw a higher moral order governing the primary world in which he lived.

Writes Randel Helms in his book, *Tolkien's World*, "Tolkien's particular myth parallels his Christianity, ... positioning a malevolent and corrupting outside influence, spiritual and probably eternal, against which man is doomed to fight, but which he has no hope of conquering" (67). Reacting to the evils of the world, Tolkien's heroes behave in an explicitly religious manner of piety: "Tolkien's hero required restrained, national as well as personal selflessness, and a concern for the good of all rather than merely the national group. [Tolkien's heroism] required the human equivalent of the selfefficacy hobbit heroism of Frodo and Sam, death to the contemporary equivalents of Boromir and, most of all, end to the desires of Sauron" (66). Thus Tolkien's heroic form is dictated primarily by the fight against evil embodied in monsters which are in their ideals radical evil; and in the world of monsters, dragons are equal to the "old serpent satan" (Helms, 3). The Balrog, Smaug, and Sauron, like the lesser monsters the hobbits encounter, are truly devils which Tolkien's heroes align themselves against, and by conquering the monsters show their adherence to the benevolence of Tolkien's Universal Will.[24]

For Tolkien, fairy stories are a form of "lower" mythology (Purtill, 13). Frodo's journey requires the carrying of a great burden and the sacrifice of self, which is similar to Christ's carrying of the cross and his crucifixion (57), but that is not to say that *The Lord of The Rings* is a religious allegory; it explicitly is not, for Tolkien almost always avoided allegories, reserving religion for the driving force of his world, but not allowing his world to act as a simple re-representation of biblical text or sermon.[25]

Briefly, what this chapter shows is that Tolkien advocates a specific and, taken together, a new type of relationship between men, nature, and religion. Embodied with his heroic æsthetic, Tolkien's Hobbit serves as a social model for Tolkien's reader.

4

A WELLSPRING OF HEROIC ENLIGHTENMENT

Before moving on to an analysis of Tolkien's three major works, *The Silmarillion* (and *The Lost Tales*, an earlier and incomplete version of the same text), *The Hobbit*, and *The Lord of the Rings*, to observe the specific advances in Tolkien's social criticism and heroic development that occurred in each, it will be useful to speak briefly of the W.P. Ker Memorial Lecture on *Sir Gawain and the Green Knight*, which Tolkien gave at the University of Glasgow, April 15th, 1953. A transcript of the essay is published in the collection, *The Monsters and the Critics and Other Essays*, edited by Tolkien's son, Christopher. What is interesting about Tolkien's critique of *Sir Gawain and the Green Knight* is that he saw the poem as explicitly involving a distinction of social code or ideology from a higher moral order, and views Gawain's actions as a servant acting faithfully for his lord as the true heroism of the poem.[26] What is important in Tolkien's approach to the poem, then, is not only that he focuses heavily on the social criticism of the *Sir Gawain and the Green Knight* poet, but also that he takes special notice of the centrality that Gawain plays within the text. Gawain, for Tolkien, is an example of the heroic servant whose actions not only rescue his lord, Arthur, from an act of *ofermod,* but also set Gawain in the role of the faithful servant who sacrifices himself for his lord and lays himself before a perceived higher morality. At the same time, Gawain, like Tidwald in Tolkien's play, distinguishes morality above his society's ideological codes.

Sir Gawain and the Green Knight begins in Camelot during Yuletide celebration between Arthur and his faithful knights, but their celebrations are interrupted by a great knight dressed all in green who challenges the court, his appearance both monstrous and majestic:

> There hurries at the hall-door an awesome master,
> the most powerful in the domain, in appearance tall,
> So square and so solid from strong neck to waist,
> Both his loins and his limbs so long and so large.
> Half monster on earth I imagined he were,
> But a man must I, nevertheless, maintain he was (Vantuono, 136-141)

The characterization of the monstrous knight continues for the next hundred or so lines before he steps forward to challenge the court of King Arthur, saying: "Who dares to strike stiffly, one stroke for another, / I shall give him as my gift this gleaming weapon, / This axe, that is heavy enough, to handle as he likes, / And I shall abide the first, my body unharmed" (287- 290). Like Unferth in *Beowulf,* the Green Knight, who appears at first a monstrous, "elvish" creation, challenges the boasts and bravery of Arthur and his court:

> 'What! Is this Arthur's house,' the knight hollered then,
> That all powers praise in principalities all over?
> Where are your great pride and past conquests,
> Your fierceness, and your fury, and your false boasts? (309-312)

The Green Knight spurs a challenge from Arthur who, acting in the chivalric code, must defend his honor. Arthur brashly accepts the Green Knight's challenge, but in so doing risks himself bodily, also risking the welfare of his entire nation. In actuality, Arthur is in a double-bind, for he must defend his honor, but the precariousness which he is allowed to put himself in (as well as the servants beneath him) and his inability to see beyond his social code is a particular weakness of the social system, and one which Tolkien believes is a specific purpose of criticism in the *Sir Gawain and the Green Knight* poem. According to Tolkien:

> "The absurdity of [the Green Knight's] challenge could not wholly be got rid of – absurdity, that is, if the story is to be conducted on a serious moral plane, in which every action of the hero, Gawain, is to be scrutinized and morally assessed – the king himself is criticized, both by the author as narrator, and by the lords of the court" (Tolkien, 75).

Gawain, though, faithfully steps forward and offers himself to the Green Knight's challenge, and it is this action of undying servitude which Tolkien values; Gawain is willing to sacrifice himself for his lord, such a sacrifice acting for the good of Gawain's society as well. Gawain interceded for Arthur:

> 'Would you, worthy lord,' said Gawain to the king
> 'Bid me step from this bench and stand by you there,
> So that I void of villainy might vacate this table,
> And if my liege lady would allow my idea,
> I would come to your counsel before your great court;
> For it seems unsuitable, as it is certainly known,
> When such a petition is presented so proudly in your hall,
> That you deign to do it, though desirous you may be,
> While many brave beings sit about upon benches' (343-351)

Like Gawain, self-sacrifice for a larger societal welfare is shown repeatedly in Sam's actions for his master, Frodo.[28] "'Let me drink first, Mr. Frodo,'" said Sam when the two have come across a watering hole in the sparseness of Mordor. "'All right, but there's room enough for two,'" responds Frodo mistaking the motivation for Sam's altruistic request. "'I didn't mean that,' said

Sam. 'I mean: if it's poisonous, or something that will show its badness quick, well, better me than you, master, if you understand me'" (RK, 242). There is the personalness of friendship in Sam's request, but there is also the awareness of the importance of the completion of the quest; Sam understands that the fate of Middle-earth relies on Frodo's destruction of the Ring, and Sam sees himself as Frodo's protector. Though Frodo, as a hobbit, is imbued with Tolkien's heroic æsthetic, he does suffer a loss of will at the final moment before he must cast the ring into the inferno, but such failure is not truly a result of *ofermod,* for Frodo has been introduced to radical evil which is beyond any man, no matter how heroic; so Frodo maintains his heroism, though he has been forever sickened by the Ring of Power.[29] Coincidentally, it can be said that Gawain suffers from a loss of will during his trial, but it might be more rightly said (as Tolkien shows through his analysis) that Gawain, like Frodo, is made even more heroic in his human frailty and necessary failure.

Tolkien views Gawain's actions as ones of true heroism:

> He takes up the challenge to rescue the king from the false position in which [Arthur's] rashness has placed him. Gawain's motive is not pride in his own prowess, not boastfulness, not even the light-hearted frivolity of knights making absurd bets and vows in the midst of the Christmas revels. His motive is a humble one: the protection of Arthur, his elder kinsman, of his king, of the head of the Round Table, from indignity and peril, and the risking instead of himself, the least of the knights (as he declares), and the one whose loss could most easily be endured. He is involved in the business, as far as it was possible to make the fairy-story go, as a matter of duty and humility and self-sacrifice (Tolkien, 74-75).

Tolkien sees this initiating act of the poem then as one of heroism on Gawain's part, and it is this faithfulness of the servant to his lord which Tolkien appreciates and develops in his fictional writings; Gawain's act is one of self sacrifice for a greater good, an act which counteracts the *ofermod* of his social superior. Frodo's decision in *The Fellowship of the Ring* during the Council of Elrond mirrors Gawain's sacrifice: "'I will take the

Ring,' [Frodo] said, 'though I do not know the way'" (264). Frodo's declaration is one of total sacrifice without a hint of personal glory, but he does not say so in response to any specific instance of *ofermod*, rather it is in response to the group turmoil which ensues in the council over the decision of what needs to be done with the Ring, and who should carry out the quest of the Ring's destruction. In part, Frodo is driven by the subtle *ofermod* of Boromir's seemingly altruistic suggestion to use the Ring in battle against Sauron:

> 'Saruman is a traitor, but did he not have a glimpse of wisdom? Why do you speak ever of hiding and destroying? Why should we not think that the Great Ring has come into our hands to serve us in the very hour of need? Wielding it the Free Lords of the Free may surely defeat the Enemy. That is what he most fears, I deem.
> 'The Men of Gondor are valiant, and they will never submit; but they may be beaten down. Valour needs first strength. Let the Ring be your weapon, if it has such power as you say. Take it and go forth to victory!' (FR, 260-261).[30]

Boromir's suggestion, in the context of Tolkien's moralistic ordering, is a dangerous one, because it seeks to obtain absolute power, even if it is for a social good. The only moral action for Tolkien (which is recognized by Frodo in the story) is the rejection of such power, and it is this rejection which Tolkien is interested in and finds so heroic; it is, specifically, a rejection of *ofermod*, or the characteristics of a person exhibiting *ofermod*, as interpreted by Tolkien. Frodo's endeavor to destroy such power is in direct opposition of the actions of characters who would wish to wield that power, because Tolkien understands that such power may never work for the benefit of society, and would only lead to social decay and destruction caused by the brash individual who believed himself capable of wielding power relegated to the realm of the gods.

Tolkien's reflections on the *Sir Gawain and the Green Knight* poem are not limited to the servitude of Gawain in his undertaking of the challenge of the Green Knight and his subsequent quest for the Green Chapel. Rather, Tolkien insists that the major actions of the poem, in the Third Fitt, focus on the temptation of Gawain, and within the temptation a demystification, or ideology laid bare, of the chivalric code. Tolkien sees Gawain as a particularly religious and penitent hero who must through the course of the poem separate his heroic code from a higher moral order to best the Green Knight. Writes Tolkien, "How does Gawain find the castle? In answer to his prayer. He has been journeying since All Hallows. It is now Christmas Eve, and he is lost in a wild strange country of tangled forest; but his chief concern is that he should not miss Mass on Christmas morning" (77). These earlier glimpses in the poem of Gawain's moral strength give special importance to the meaning of his failure in the chivalric code: specifically, Gawain, through religious piety, is given the vision of a higher order, and thus may transgress his social ideology (when he lies to Bertilak).

At the Castle Perilous Gawain encounters his second trial, one which tests both Gawain's morality and heroic code; Gawain is tempted, and through his temptation he is forced to transgress his chivalric code, yet maintains his higher morality. The master of the castle says to Gawain:

> Whatever I win in the woods will pass on to you,
> and what gains you garner you must give to me.
> Thus shall we swap, sweet knight, having sworn with honor,
> Whatever, sir, will occur, the worse or the better.
> (Vantuono, 1106-1109)

Gawain agrees to the bargain and for the next two days, while the master is away hunting in the woods, Gawain is tempted by the master's lady: "There are many ladies who would be more desirous now / To have you, handsome man, in their hold, as I have you here, / To dally thus dearly with your delightful words, / Recover their comfort and cool their cares, Than much of the goods or gold gained by them ever" (1251-1255). All Gawain allows himself to exchange with the fair lady the first two nights are two kisses which he exchanges for the prizes from the master's hunt, as was the agreement between the two men. On the third night, however, the lady of the castle offers Gawain a green girdle which she says will protect its wearer from any harm. Here is the talisman Gawain needs to defeat the magical and monstrous Green Knight, the whereabouts of whom the master knows and has agreed to take Gawain to after his three nights at the castle are up. On the evening of the third day Gawain is untruthful to the master, concealing the gift of the green girdle from him.[31]

Tolkien insists that Gawain's concealment of the girdle is not a moral failure, rather recognition of a higher order of morality and justification over his chivalric code, which Gawain has breached with his concealment of the gift. Writes Tolkien,

> Gawain in his perilous extremity was obliged to tear his 'code' in two, and distinguish its components of good manners and good morals... We have in fact reached the intersection of two different planes: of a real and permanent, and an unreal and passing world of values: morals on the one hand, and on the other a code of honour, or a game with rules. The personal code of most people was, and of many still is, like that of Sir Gawain made up of a close blend of the two. (89)

Gawain's actions, then, reflect critically on the chivalric code, and offer a subtle criticism for the close reader of the social ideology of that time. Importantly, Tolkien recognizes this; in fact it is his central focus of the lecture he gave on the poem, and undoubtedly this emphasis on the social criticism which the poem entails influenced the direction of Tolkien's own writing. Even though Gawain's untruthfulness is revealed (for as it turns out the Green Knight and the master of the Castle Perilous are one and the same), Gawain still remains true to his morality. Moreover, following Tolkien's interpretation, it is specifically heroic of Gawain that he recognizes and transgresses what is revealed to be a flawed social system occurring within the chivalric order.

Sir Gawain and the Green Knight's importance to Tolkien's development of social criticism in his works of fiction, as revealed through Tolkien's lecture on the poem, are twofold. Firstly, Tolkien recognizes the heroism of Gawain's actions to save Arthur from unnecessary danger; Gawain is Tolkien's servant hero aligned with a higher moral truth, but unlike such figures as seen in *Beowulf*,[32] Gawain is given the central action of the poem. *Sir Gawain and the Green Knight* then embodies a Middle English text in which the servant figure is given the centrality of the narrative, though to some degree it must be recognized that Gawain was not a true servant figure, but rather a prestigious knight acting in service to a divinely sanctioned king; Tolkien would take the process a step further, focusing on what would have been Gawain's squire or page, a character best exemplified in Sam Gamgee.

The second major importance of Tolkien's interpretation of *Sir Gawain and the Green Knight* is the focus on social criticism, and Tolkien's interpretation that the *Sir Gawain and the Green Knight* poet was making an explicit distinction between a social code and a higher morality. Such observation deconstructed the chivalric code, and honored Gawain for transgressing what is revealed as flawed social ideology. With this recognition, Tolkien hoped to achieve the same purpose; his hobbits are similar to Gawain, for they are humble and servile. In the context of Tolkien's divine providence they embody ideals which Tolkien associated with a morality given to the design of a higher order. Like Gawain, Tolkien's hobbits are meant to serve as social models for an age in which the social system is viewed as degenerative by the author, and the moralistic hobbits as guides for the reclamation of a proper social order.

5

TOLKIEN'S DEVELOPING HEROICS

The Tale of Turin Son of Húrin (Or Urin, as he is named in *The Book Of Lost Tales*), begun by Tolkien his senior year as an undergraduate at Oxford, is the oldest in Tolkien's collection of tales intended to serve as a collective mythology for England, a project never completed, but one which was published posthumously by Christopher Tolkien as *The Silmarillion*. Tolkien would return to the tale of Turin repeatedly during his lifetime, and there are now more than five versions of the story in print.33 None of these retellings represent a completed version of Turin's story, but they do signify, as stipulated by Richard C. West in his essay, "Turin's Ofermod: An Old English Theme in the Development of the Story of Turin," a development of social criticism in Tolkien's original story, specifically focusing on the *ofermod* which Tolkien recognizes in Beorhtnoth in *The Battle of Maldon* and applied to his character Turin.

Christopher Tolkien wrote on the Tale of Turin that it was "in some respects the most tangled and complex of all the narrative elements in the story of the First Age" (UT, 6). Turin's tale originally represented for Tolkien a retelling of the story of the fateful hero Kullervo from the Finnish folklore epic, the *Kalevala*.

Tolkien wrote in October 1914 to his future wife, Edith Bratt: "Among other work I am trying to turn one of the stories [of the *Kalevala*] – which is really a very great story and most tragic – into a short story somewhat on the lines of [William] Morris's romances with chunks of poetry in between" (Carpenter, 7). On July 16, 1864, Tolkien wrote to Christopher Bretherton:

> The germ of my attempt to write legends of my own to fit my private languages was the tragic tale of the hapless Kullervo in the Finnish *Kalevala*. It remains a major matter in the legends of the First Age (which I hope to publish as The Silmarillion), though as 'The Children of Húrin' it is entirely changed except in the tragic endings (Carpenter, 345).

Quite possibly, Tolkien found the tale of Kullervo so appealing because of the association he found with the personal tragedy of the hero. The story of Kullervo involves a family feud and the separation of a son from his parents.[34] Similar actions play out in Tolkien's tale, but Turin's strife is more than a mirroring of the original Finnish source, rather the *Kalevala* served as a stepping block which Tolkien used initially but diverged from greatly in his own tale. It should also be mentioned that Glaurung the dragon, the primary adversary of Turin (besides Turin's own actions) and Turin's counterpart, is explicitly not from the *Kalevala*, but rather gathered from the Norse legends, the *Niblungenlied*, the *Volsungasaga*, and to some small extent *Beowulf*. Glaurung is an important character when considering Turin's *ofermod;* for Glaurung is not simply an adversary, but a powerful general of unchecked power and will, a creature who both exhibits *ofermod* and is a representation of *ofermod* in its raw self, and thus reflects upon Turin – the two are very similar indeed.

In the character of Turin there is an ever increasing use of Anglo-Saxon *ofermod* as Tolkien interpreted the word in *The Battle of Maldon*. A study of Turin's transformations, such as the one West gives in his essay, shows Tolkien's increasing interest in the heroic code and its social reflections. Specifically, West identifies a change in the focus of the underlying actions which motivate the darkly heroic Turin (or Turambar, "escaper of fate," as he so renames himself in the original tale), from an evil spell of Fate cast by Melko (Morgoth) and used as revenge upon Húrin,[35] to the unchecked pride and violence of Turin's *ofermod*. Writes West, "I believe that this tension between bravery and foolhardiness becomes a major leitmotif in [Tolkien's] Saga of Turin as it developed, though it was not what initially drew him to the story, the first of all his tales of Middle-earth" (236).

Turin, like his Finnish counterpart (and like Tolkien himself), is separated from his parents at a very early age. He is seven when his mother, Mavwin, sends him from Hithlum to the court of Tinwelint; this is before Turin's sister, Nienori is born (which will play into Turin's bad fortune by the conclusion of Tolkien's story). While living with the elves, Turin becomes a great warrior, but he is cursed by Melkor, and has Melkor's wrath of war in his actions:

> To ease his sorrow and the rage of his heart, that remembered always how Urin (or Húrin) and his folk had gone down in battle against Melko, Turin was for ever ranging with the most warlike of the folk of Tinwelint far abroad, and long ere he was grown to first manhood he slew and took hurts in frays with the Orcs that prowled unceasingly upon the confines of the realm and were a menace to the Elves (LT, 74).

Turin flees the courts of Tinwelint, though, after in a fit of rage he kills an elf, Orgof, who has been taunting Turin both about the loss of his mother and his ill-kept appearance:

> Then a fierce anger born of his sore heart and these words concerning the lady Mavwin blazed suddenly in Turin's breast, so that he seized a heavy drinking-vessel of gold that lay by his right hand and unmindful of his strength he cast it with great force in Orgof's teeth, saying: 'Stop thy mouth therewith, fool, and prate no more.' But Orgof's face was broken and he fell back with a great weight...for he was dead (75).

Thinking that he has become an outlaw, Turin ranges the

land alone, save for one close companion, an elf named Beleg.

Turin's initial actions can not truly be said to be entirely reflective of *ofermod*, for they are tied closely with Melko's curse and an inescapable fate, but also because Turin's actions only increase his own ill fortune and do not damn innocent people dependent upon him for their welfare. Turin, at this stage, mirrors Beowulf before he becomes king; both authors reflect on attributes of over-action or zeal in the characters of the men, but such action does not truly become *ofermod* until they are elevated to lords over the people.

West reflects upon Turin's development in the version of the story found in *Unfinished Tales*,

> Melian calls him 'over-bold' and counsels him to 'fear both the heat and the cold of your heart' (UT, 79). He is never able to attain this moderation. Bereft of his father while a child, raised to think of himself as heir to the lordship of Dor-lómin while the realm is overrun by invaders... he naturally grows into a fierce and redoubtable warrior, and a lonely, isolated man, sensitive in matters of honor. He is proud, arrogant and self-willed. The Anglo-Saxons might have called him *ofermodig* (242- 243).

Importantly, not only does West recognize the criticism of *ofermod* within Turin's character, but he observes as well that there is a continual development of a more complexly thought-out social criticism into the successive retellings of the tale; Turin's actions become more and more that of a brash leader who harms not only himself but the society which is dependent upon his rule. West recounts the point in Turin's story after he has accidentally slain his companion, Beleg, and returned home searching for his mother, only to find Mavwin gone, her home and livestock taken over by Brodda. In a rage, Turin slays Brodda, but the extent of his destruction varies in each version of the story:

> The early version of 'Turumbar' does not have this wholesale slaughter (only Brodda himself and one defender are killed) (LT, 90-91), nor Aerin's (Brodda's wife) self immolation (rather she gets her

nephew safely away)... Tolkien has gradually added all of that, the better to exemplify Turin's pride and wrath, and their consequences (243).

Even in the earlier version, however, Turin's actions at this point begin to exhibit the true *ofermod* found in Beorhtnoth in *The Battle of Maldon* poem. In Turin's wrath, not only does he slay Brodda, but a hall companion as well, Orlin, who had no conflict with Turin. Aerin calls Turin's actions "violent and unlawful," exhibiting Turin's social failure, and Turin's actions only succeed in his banishment from society and the loss of Mavwin's possessions as retribution to the spouse of the slain man: "those lands and goods that were Urin's shall Brodda's kin hold, save only do Mavwin and Nienori return ever from their wandering. Yet even so may Turin son of Urin inherit nor part nor parcel of them ever" (LT, 90-91). In this exchange, Turin's actions are pointless but begin to exhibit the larger social ramifications caused by the over-brashness of a lord. His recklessness doesn't allow him to reclaim his mother's possessions, rather he forfeits his inheritance, which is given over to Aerin unless Marvwin and her daughter, Nienori, should return.

An even stronger example of Turin's growing *ofermod* in the original telling of the story occurs earlier, after Turin has joined a band of elves led by Orodreth. Though Turin is not yet a leader of the people, his great ferocity in battle draws the attention of Melkor, who sends hosts of evil, led by the dragon, or Foaloke (as he is called in the story), Glorund:

> By Turin's deeds however was the ancient counsel of the Rodothlim set aside and their abode made known far and wide, nor was Melko ignorant of it, yet many of the Noldoli now fled to them and their strength waxed and Turin was held in great honor among them... while Melko gathered in secret his great hordes. These did he loose suddenly upon them at unawares, and they gathered their warriors in great haste and went against him, but behold, an army of Orcs descended upon them, and wolves, and Orcs mounted upon wolves; and a great worm was with them whose scales were polished bronze and whose breath was a mingled fire and smoke, and his name was

Glorund. All men of the Rodothlim fell or were taken in that battle (LT, 84).

The aftermath of the battle puts special emphasis on Turin's overreaching brashness as the cause for the destruction of the Rodothlim: "There died Orodreth, reproaching Turin that he had ever withstood his wise counsels, and Turin's heart was bitter at the ruin of the folk that was set to his account" (84). Here Turin's actions are far reaching, the catalyst for the destruction of a people, the first great tragedy of the story attributed to Turin, and may truly be considered under Tolkien's interpretation of *ofermod*.

Glorund is more than the mindless beast in the story, rather he is an integral part of Melkor's plans to ruin Turin as revenge against Húrin. Glorund can speak and with his very gaze cast a spell over those who look upon him. He is a great and powerful general of the enemy and as such exhibits, strangely, his own *ofermod*:

> Thus was it that this *loke* (for so the Eldar named the worms of Melkor) suffered the Orcs to slay whom they would and to gather whom they listed into a very great and very sorrowful throng of women, maids, and little children, but all the mighty treasure that they had brought from the rocky halls and heaped glistering in the sun before the doors he coveted for himself and forbade them set finger on it, and they durst not withstand him (LT, 85).

Turin too is brought before Glorund's dark majesty and is laid helpless before the dragon; but such helplessness has metaphoric meaning as well, for Glorund is raw anger and spite, and the uncontrolled emotion which Turin exhibits through his bloodlust. Turin's inability to gain control over himself before Glorund represents in part his inability to control his raw emotions, and the power such uncontrolled emotions have over his actions. Thus Glorund is the embodiment of Turin's *ofermod*, Turin's destruction:

> Turin was held by the spell of the drake, for that beast had a foul

magic in his glance, as have many others of his kindred, and he turned the sinews of Turin as it were to stone, for his eye held Turin's eye so that his will died, and he could not stir of his own purpose, yet might he see and hear (LT 86).

Glorund serves as a keystone in Melko's plot against Turin, and as an indomitable will which Turin can not overcome, a will that is reflective of Turin's own actions. If such is the case, then Turin's doom cannot be attributed entirely to the curse placed upon him by Melko; rather, Turin must be held accountable for his actions, for in the clash of wills, Turin is able to recover himself from the dragon's spellbinding stare and thus proclaims, "'Nay, from this hour shall none name me Turin if I live. Behold, I will name me a new name and it shall be Turambar!'" (86). The question of Melko's spell over Turin is problematic, for if it is accepted as the justification of Turin's actions, then Turin's *ofermod* is not that at all, but rather the result of the curse of malevolent will laid upon him. West disagrees with such an assessment and believes rather that such fatalistic beliefs are but another social criticism of Tolkien's placed upon Anglo-Saxon heroism. Writes West,

> Much of Tolkien's œuvre deals with the operation of fate and free will, chance and luck and coincidence and Providence, and the many shades of meaning in the word doom (which encapsulates all of those themes). He prefers to recount events suggestive of all these possibilities without committing himself to any explanation, and particularly not a simple one. Morgoth's influence is indeed pervasive and subtle, but individuals have motivations for their actions...
> Turin is like his contemporaries in tending to blame Morgoth's [Melko's] curse for his troubles, even frequently changing or concealing his name to deflect it; and the malice of that fallen Valar does create hard circumstances that blight his life. He is in a long line of mythic figures who bring about their fate by trying to avoid it (242).

The fatalistic nature of Turin remains problematic for the effectiveness of Tolkien's social criticism and application of *ofermod*, for Melko's curse is a very real threat; Melko is an active participant in Middle-earth at this time, and his account of what will befall Húrin's son works as the opening exchange of the story; Melko is not some distant, mythical threat. The curse upon Turin is immediate, occurring when he is alive and not some decades beforehand. The only thing certain about the problematic framing of fate into Turin's actions is that it lessens the strength of Tolkien's social criticism; the tale shows Turin acting out of what may be defined as *ofermod,* but the source of that *ofermod* is ill-defined. Does Turin act out of his own will or does an evil, dominating power drive his actions? Such is the problematic question struck in this earlier tale, and it shows Tolkien's social criticism in a stage of early development.

As Turin's story proceeds, Mavwin journeys with Nienori in search of her lost son. She reaches the courts of Tinwelint where it is suspected that Turin is held among Glorung's horde. Together with a band of warriors, Mavwin and Nienori travel to Glorung's lair hoping to find Turin alive, but Glorung slaughters the elven warriors and (acting as Melko's agent) casts a spell of forgetfulness upon Nienori who runs lost through the woods. She happens across a wanderer: "Wild and black was his hair yet streaked with grey, and his face was pale and marked as with deep sorrows of the past, and in his hand he bare a great sword whereof all but the very edge was black" (99); it is Turin, her lost brother, but neither sibling recognizes the other, and Nienori has forgotten herself through Glorung's curse. Turin names his sister Niniel. Here the narrative is closest to mirroring Kullervo's tale in the *Kalevala,* with the introduction of unknowing incest between brother and sister.[36]

Turin and Nienori marry and Turin is named chief of his people. Now he is truly responsible for actions of *ofermod* and in the concluding events of the story there is a great similarity with Beowulf, for Turin goes on to slay Glorund; many of his band flee leaving only six warriors to stand with him against Glorund, the dragon. Hiding stealthily in a crack of the earth, Turin waits for Glorund to pass over him, then (like Sigimund) strikes upward at the unprotected belly, using his blade, the bloodthirsty Gurtholfin, to slice open the dragon's under-pelt:

> Then abiding until a very vital and unfended spot was within stroke, he heaved up Gutholfin his black sword and stabbed with all his strength above his head, and that magic blade of the Rodothlim [the dead lord Orodreth made Turin the blade] went into the vitals of the dragon even to the hilt, and the yell of his death-pain rent the woods and all that heard it were aghast (LT, 107).

Turin succeeds in the slaying of the beast but swoons as if dead beside his fallen foe. When Nienori comes to his side she thinks him lost; Glorung speaks his dying words to her, which awakens her from the spell of forgetfulness he placed upon her and completes Melko's fateful plans against Turin, and Húrin through him:

> 'o though Nienori daughter of Mavwin, I give thee joy that thou has found thy brother at last, for the search has been weary – and now is he become very mighty fellow and a stabber of his foes unseen'; but Nienori sat as if one stunned, and with that Glorund died, and with his death the veil of his spells fell from her, and all her memory grew crystal clear (109).

Learning of her incest, like Kullervo's sister, she casts herself into the Silver Bowl, a raging river, where she drowns. Turin, awaking, searches for her, and is told by Tamar the Lame (who wished Nienori for his own, and who overheard Glorung's words to her) the truth of what has transpired. Enraged, Turin slays Tamar, then thrusts himself (like Kullervo) upon his blade, Gurtholfin:

> 'Hail, Gurtholfin, wand of death, for thou art all men's bane and all men's lives fain wouldst thou drink, knowing no lord or faith save the hand that wields thee if it be strong. Thee only have I now – slay me therefore and be swift, for life is a curse, and all my days are creeping foul, and all my deeds are vile, and all I love is dead.' And Gurtholfin said: 'That will I gladly do, for blood is blood, and perchance thine is not less sweet than many a one's that thou hast given me ere now'; and Turambar cast himself then upon the point of Gurtholfin, and the dark blade took his life (LT, 112).

Turin is finally consumed by his hatred and bloodshed; in slaying Glorung he brings about Melko's fate and the death of his sister, and his suicide. His speaking blade is representative of his own insatiable thirst for violence; Gurtholfin, Turin's bloodthirstiness, destroys Glorung and Turin equally, binding the two in a bloody pact of *ofermod*, both leaving the subordinates under them to the perils of the world. Though nothing is said of Turin's people, they are left leaderless and vulnerable through Turin's final, brash act of *ofermod*; Like the Geats at the end of Beowulf, they are open to the invasion of enemy nations and monster hordes:

> With heavy spirits
> They mourned their despair, the death of their lord;
> and a sorrowful song sang the Geatish woman,
> with hair bound up, for Beowulf the king,
> with sad cares, earnestly said
> that she dreaded the hard days ahead,
> the times of slaughter, the host's terror,
> harm and captivity. Heaven swallowed the smoke (3148b-3155)

The *Tale of Turambar and The Foaloke* is important because it shows an early point in Tolkien's development of social criticism. Tolkien's *ofermod* is mingled with the wrathfulness of Melko and the curse placed upon Turin. In the aftermath of the story, however, it is said Turin ascends to the heavens and will have final revenge upon Melko (Morgoth): "Turumbar indeed shall stand beside Finwë in the Great Wrack, and Melko and his drakes shall curse the sword of Mormakil" (116). Such a statement confuses the matter of Turin's *ofermod*, for Turin is given a saintly status. Like *The Battle of Maldon* scribe, Tolkien is at best giving a criticism of the heroic code, but has yet to give answer to it or apply it to his time. As West postulates, as Tolkien returns to the tale over the years, the social criticism through *ofermod* may increase, yet there is little Tolkien could do (without major rewriting) to make Turin's tale relevant to his age, since Turin himself is not representative of Tolkien's heroic æsthetic. At best, Turin, full of rage and vengeful, is an oversimplification of the matter of Anglo-Saxon *ofermod;* his character can be seen as a mere allegory of the brashness of *ofermod* (though this was obviously not Tolkien's intention), for he does not contain any subtleties of character.

The "Tale of Turin" is a beautifully tragic story masterfully told (and I am glad to see the latest version finally released in *The Children of Húrin*), but it is without Tolkien's hero; Turin is of nobility and neither meek nor penitent; he actively seeks out monsters and violence. In these regards, Turin's actions mirror Anglo-Saxon heroism, but Tolkien has added an especially strong critique of *ofermod* to his character. Whether or not that *ofermod* can be attributed to his will alone is especially problematic to the social significance of the story, which in itself is already limited by the nature of Tolkien's choice for his central character. Most importantly Tolkien had yet to introduce his own brand of heroism into the narrative; Bilbo and Frodo and the hobbits were not yet part of Middle-earth.

Like Turin's story, the "Tale of Beren and Lúthien" went through multiple revisions, drafts, and publications, but Beren presents a very different heroic type than Turin (Though certainly Beren does not exhibit Tolkien's ultimate heroism imbued in his hobbits.); and yet Beren still suffers from a blind adherence to the ideals of a flawed code of honor. Indeed, his actions are consistently opposite to the observations made by Gawain of a higher moral order placed above his chivalric code. For the intent of this study, West's original interpretations of a graduation of greater social criticism in the later drafts of Tolkien's successive retelling may be applied to the Tale of Beren and Lúthien, though, as in the "Tale of Turin," certain shortcomings must be considered when analyzing this tale for the merits of its social criticism.

The original version of the romance of Beren and Lúthien tale is the *Tale of Tinúviel* and dates back to 1917 (though the original text was literally erased by Tolkien as he made revisions); the tale is printed *in The Book of Lost Tales Book Two*, edited by Christopher Tolkien, and in a much condensed and revised version in *The Silmarillion*. The story is of great interest because of, in part, the anomaly it represents in Tolkien's heroic æsthetic, since this is the only one of Tolkien's greater stories to focus specifically on a romantic quest and the undying love between a man and a woman. Originally, both Beren and Lúthien (then named Tinúviel) were elves, but in the later version of *The Silmarillion, Of Beren and Lúthien*, Beren is a man and a great warrior, the son of Barahir, and a bold outlaw who singlehandedly torments Melko and his hoards. In the later version of the tale, greater emphasis is put upon the development of Beren's origins and heroic actions; like Turin, he is the heir to a destroyed nation, the Men of Dorthonion. Greater emphasis is also put upon the character of Huan, the heroic hound, who helps Lúthien save Beren from the Sauron's dungeon and later battles against the were-wolf Carcharoth, the Red Maw; Huan, it will be shown, is a true hero of the tale who, unlike Beren and like Gawain, distinguishes between social ideals and a higher morality.

In Tolkien's original telling, Beren is a member of the elves, the Noldoli, who under Fëanor left the Valar, the far west and land of the gods. A rift had occurred between the elves through Fëanor's kinslaying of the Teleri and the separation upon the western road; many elves stayed in Middle-earth when the gods called them westward, and these were named the Ilkorindi (or Lost Elves), "which is to say Eldar [or elves] that never had beheld Valinor or the Two trees or dwelt in Kor" (LT 9). Lúthien (or Tinúviel as she is originally named) is the daughter of the king and queen of the Lost Elves (Tinwelint and Gwending in *Lost Tales*, Thingol and Melian in *The Silmarillion*). Beren, wandering alone in the woods, spies Lúthien dancing majestically and is immediately smitten:

> Yet now did he see Tinúviel dancing in the twilight, and Tinúviel was in a Silver-pearly dress, and her bare white feet were twinkling among

the hemlock-stems. Then Beren cared not whether she were Vala or Elf or child of Men and crept near to see; and he leant against a young elm that grew upon a mound so that he might look down into the little glade where she was dancing, for the enchantment made him faint (LT,11).

Lúthien comes to love Beren, but when the romance is revealed to Thingol, he will not allow it and sends Beren on a seemingly impossible quest:

'I see the ring, son of Barahir, and I perceive that you are proud, and deem yourself mighty... Yet you say that bonds such as these do not daunt you. Go your way therefore! Bring to me in your hand a Simaril from Morgoth's crown; and then, if she will, Lúthien may set her hand in yours. Then you shall have my jewel; and though the fate of Arda lies within the Silmarils, yet you shall hold me generous (Sil, 167).

Beren agrees to Thingol's demands, but in his brash acceptance and doggedness to complete Thingol's unreasonable request there is a blindness exhibited in the inability to situate higher morality above a social code. In both tellings of the tale, Beren's actions, socially mystified and notably unlike Gawain's, jeopardize his and Lúthien's safety and happiness, and in the later version of the telling there is an added deeper criticism of Beren's inability to prescribe higher importance to Lúthien's wishes and a higher ordering of love in his persistence to fulfill his oath to Thingol. Speaks Lúthien to Beren,

'You must choose, Beren, between these two: to relinquish the quest and your oath and seek a life of wandering upon the face of the earth; or to hold to your word and challenge the power of darkness upon its throne. But on either road I shall go with you, and our doom shall be alike' (Sil, 177).

Lúthien has offered her devotion to Beren and there is no need therefore for him to risk himself with the acquisition of the Silmaril. Not only has Lúthien told Beren as much, but she also has told him that her fate is tied now with his; she will faithfully follow him, so in his brashness to continue his quest he is risking not only his life but Lúthien's as well. To be fair, Beren like

Arthur in *Sir Gawain and the Green Knight,* is caught in a double-bind, for he either must operate within the social code and in doing so risk Lúthien and her love, or forsake society and become an outcast. Later, Beren seems to recognize the dangerous position he is placing Lúthien in, but is unable to listen to his reasoning. The wise Huan tells him as much. Speaks Húrin first then Huan:

> 'Thrice now I curse my oath to Thingol,' he said, 'and I would that he had slain me in Menegroth, rather than I should bring you [Lúthien] under the shadow of Morgoth.'
> Then for a second time Huan spoke with words; and he counseled Beren saying: 'From the shadow of death you can no longer save Lúthien, for by her love she is now subject to it. You can turn from your fate and lead her into exile, seeking peace in vain while your life lasts. But if you will not deny your doom, then either Lúthien, being forsaken, must assuredly die alone, or she must with you challenge the fate that lies before you – hopeless, yet not certain.' (Sil, 179).

Beren has committed himself to the quest and Lúthien to him: he to a social code, and her to a higher morality; Huan alludes to the fact that she has forsaken her immortality as an elf and will become mortal through her love for Beren – a great sacrifice. Lúthien then must be seen through her undying and unquestioning love as a figure of heroic servitude who not only forsakes her safety for Beren, but also, as the tale unfolds, saves Beren from the outcome of his brash actions of *ofermod*, while Beren, in his ineptitude and rage, becomes subject to Morgoth's wrath. When compared to the Tale of Turin, Beren and Lúthien's tale begins to provide an answer to the nature of Tolkien's *ofermod* through a subtle development of subservient heroes, which both Lúthien and Huan represent.

Beren on his heroic quest seeks out Melko (Morgoth) but is captured by an Orc raiding party and brought before the dark lord. Through an act of cunning Beren says that he came seeking the employment of Melko: "Many a great tale wherefore, albeit I am no renegade thrall, I do desire nothing so much as to serve thee in what small manner I may" (LT, 15). The act of guile saves his life but he is made a thrall of Tevildo, Prince of Cats.[37]

In *The Silmarillion's* version there is a greater development of Beren's questing actions before he is made a servant to Sauron: He ventures into the courts of King Finrod Felegund, Finarfin's son, and nephew to the over-bold Fëanor, the creator of the Silmarils. Finrod and a band of elves become Beren's traveling companions, and through Finrod, Beren's unjustified quest, and Thingol's deeper purposes are made apparent:

> 'It is plain that Thingol desires your death; but it seems that this doom goes beyond his purpose, and that the Oath of Fëanor is again at work. For the Silmarils are cursed with an oath of hatred, and he that even names them in desire moves a great power from slumber; and the sons of Fëanor would lay all the Elf-kingdoms in ruin rather than suffer any other than themselves to win or possess a Silmaril, for the oath drives them.' (169)

In the later tale, Thingol's alternate purpose (other than the disposal of Beren at Melko's wrath) is made plain, and Beren is made into an agent of a lord hoping to gain absolute power. Beren would be wise then to abandon the quest for he is acting as an agent to bring corrupted power to Thingol, but he holds to his code of honor, again valuing a social æsthetic above a higher moral order, and again failing, unlike Gawain (and specifically through Tolkien's interpretation of heroism in the decisions and moral ordering of the knight), to recognize a stratification of morality and importance within his value system. Felegund accompanies Beren only to be imprisoned with him in the dungeons of Sauron, where Felegund, acting heroically, sacrifices himself in a fight with a werewolf to save Beren: "But when the wolf came for Beren, Felegund put forth all his power, and burst his bonds; and he wrestled with the werewolf, and slew it with his hands and teeth; yet he himself was wounded to the death" (Sil, 174).

In both versions of the tale, Lúthien (Tinúviel) is imprisoned in a high tree by Thingol to keep her from searching out Beren, but through her magical craft of song escapes to find Beren enthralled in Sauron's (Telvido's) courts.38 Escaping her imprisonment, Lúthien risks her own safety and uses her spellbinding songs to free Beren from Sauron's thralldom. Huan (the other truly heroic figure of the tale), recognizes the goodness in her higher morality and serves Lúthien. In Lúthien's sacrifice of self, she recognizes the moral virtue of love as higher than a social code which would keep her subservient to her lord and father, Thingol, and repeatedly sacrifices herself for Beren, while Beren, unable to ignore his chivalric duty, puts Lúthien in unnecessary danger:

> Beren, being torn between his oath and his love, and knowing Lúthien to be now safe, arose one morning before the sun, and committed her to the care of Huan; then in great anguish he departed while she yet slept upon the grass... But Lúthien heard his song, and she sang in answer, as she came through the woods unlooked for. (Sil, 178)

And again it is through Lúthien's spell craft that Beren receives the Silmaril from Morgoth's crown:

> Morgoth looking upon her beauty conceived in his thought an evil lust, and a design more dark than any had yet come into his heart since he fled from Valinor. Thus he was beguiled by his own malice, for he watched her leaving her free for a while, and taking a secret pleasure in his thought. Then suddenly she eluded his sight, and out of the shadows began a song of such surpassing loveliness, and of such blinding power, that he listened perforce; and a blindness came upon him, as his eyes roamed to and fro, seeking her (Sil, 180).

Lúthien's power is embodied through her song, and through the higher morality of her soul she is able to conquer Morgoth, allowing Beren the chance to pry a Silmaril from Morgoth's crown, fulfilling his quest to Thingol; but Beren is ultimately maimed by the werewolf guardian of Morgoth, Carcharoth, who devours Beren's hand and the Silmaril held there in, the action serving as a final and startling criticism of Beren's actions, and the subsequent ravaging of Carcharoth into Thingol's realm exemplifying the king's responsibility in Beren's actions (and through them endangerment of his own daughter and people). The ravaging of Carcharoth also serves to illustrate the inevitable failure in trying to obtain the corrupted power of the Silmarils, since they were made through the *ofermod* of Fëanor. Carcharoth's actions are similar to Grendel's in this regard, both monsters serving to criticize the societies they attack and infest:

> But in the north of [Thingol's] realm his messengers met with a peril sudden and unlooked for: the onslaught of Carcharoth, the Wolf of Angband. In his madness he had run ravening from the north, and passing at length over Taur-nu-Fuin upon its eastern side he came down from the sources of Esgalduin like a destroying fire... For fate drove him, and the power of the Silmaril that he bore to his torment. Thus he burst into the inviolate woods of Doriath, and all fled away in fear (Sil, 184).

Carcharoth's plague of Thingol's domain is the ultimate end to a corrupted quest, brought about by Beren's adherence to his code of honor. And it is great irony when Thingol asks: "'What of your quest, and of your vow?'" Beren responds by holding up his right arm, showing the mangled stub for which he has renamed himself Camlost, the Empty-handed; for indeed Beren has fulfilled his quest: his hand and the Silmaril rest in the fiery-pit inside Carcharoth, the enraged beast tormenting Thingol's domain through the Silmaril embedded within its stomach.

The character of Huan undergoes the most significant change between the earliest existent version of the tale and the version found in *The Silmarillion*. In *Tinúviel*, Huan is described simply as "Huan Captain of the Dogs" who is Tevildo's, the Prince of Cats', greatest enemy. In this version, Huan aids Lúthien by fighting off Telvido and later slaying Karkaras (Carcharoth), with Beren's help, after the werewolf has bitten off Beren's hand:

> Then Beren thrust swiftly upward with a spear into his throat, and Huan leapt again and had him by a hind leg, and Karkaras fell as a stone, for at that same moment the king's spear found his heart, and his evil spirit gushed forth and sped howling faintly as it fared over the dark hills to Mandos; but Beren lay under him crushed beneath his weight (LT, 39).

Already in this early version of the tale, Huan is depicted as a heroic character in servitude to Lúthien; his actions are ennobled because he recognizes the virtue in Lúthien's love for Beren and her altruistic actions to aid her lover. Huan, however, is given little development as a secondary figure involved in a story centered on Beren and Lúthien. In the final retelling, however, Huan is given central action and the greatest heroisms are attributed to him, while, like Tolkien's interpretation of Gawain, Huan is given a deeper moral reflection and forced to choose between a social code and a higher moral order.

In *Of Beren and Lúthien*, chapter nineteen of *The Silmarillion*, Huan is in the service of Celegorm and Curfin, the offspring of Fëanor who, through Fëanor's kinslaying and *ofermod* are subject to Mandos' curse placed upon Fëanor's bloodline. Through a brief historical reflection, insight is given to Huan's origins:

> Now the chief of the wolfhounds that followed Celegorm was named Huan. He was not born in Middle-earth, but came from the Blessed Realm; for Orome had given him to Celegorm long ago in Valinor, and there he had followed the horn of his master, before evil came. Huan followed Celegorm into exile, and was faithful; and thus he too came under the doom of woe set upon the Noldor, and it was decreed that he should meet death, but not until he encountered the mightiest wolf that would ever walk the world (Sil, 173).

Acting faithfully toward his master, Huan retrieves Lúthien for Celegorm who "believing that Beren and Felegund were prisoners beyond hope of aid," wished Lúthien for himself to marry. However, when Huan finds out his master's corrupted plans for Lúthien, he is able to distinguish a higher moral ordering than a fidelity to his corrupted lord and helps Lúthien escape:

> But Huan the hound was true of heart, and the love of Lúthien had fallen upon him in the first hour of their meeting; and he grieved at her captivity...
> Now Huan devised a plan for the aid of Lúthien; and coming at a time of night he brought her cloak, and for the first time he spoke,

> giving her counsel. Then he led her by secret out of Nargothrond, and they fled north together; and he humbled his pride and suffered her to ride upon him in the fashion of a steed. (Sil, 173)

In his actions, Huan is not only emblematic of an enlightened hero, distinguishing between social ideology and moral superiority (much in the same way as Tolkien sees Gawain), but he is also the first instance of Tolkien's heroic layering: Huan is a humble servant to Lúthien who herself is loyal to Beren. Huan is an early representation of the Sam figure, a servant to a servant; this is an important development in Tolkien's narrative. Already Tolkien is giving over more of his narrative to his servant figure and moving beyond the *Gawain* poet by placing heroic emphasis on both the servant and the servant of the servant, but Tolkien has yet to imbue his heroes with his heroic æsthetic, as he will do in the creation of the Hobbit. Huan's heroism can not be understated however, for even when he is face to face with Sauron, he is victorious:

> But no wizardry nor spell, neither fang nor venom, nor devil's art nor Beast-strength could overthrow Huan of Valinor; and he took his foe by the throat and pinned him down. Then Sauron shifted shape, but he could not elude the grip of Huan without forsaking his body utterly...
> Then Sauron yielded himself, and Lúthien took the mastery of the isle and all that was there; and Huan released him. And immediately he took the form of a vampire, great as a dark cloud across the moon, and he fled, dripping blood from his throat upon the trees, and came to Taur-nu-Fuin, and dwelt there, filling it with horror. (Sil, 175)

Only when Huan confronts Carcharoth is his heroism matched with the *ofermod* of Thingol represented in the werewolf's rage; and so Huan's doom, wrought by the *ofermod* of Fëanor (the initiating *ofermod* of the elves and races of Middle-earth) is fulfilled:

> Huan in that hour slew Carcharoth; but there in the woven woods of Doriath his own doom long spoken was fulfilled, and he was wounded mortally, and the venom of Morgoth entered into him. Then he came, and falling beside Beren spoke for the third time with

> words; and he bade Beren farewell before he died. Beren spoke not, but laid his hand upon the head of the hound, and so they parted (Sil, 186).

The "Tale of Beren and Lúthien" thus exhibits several important advances in Tolkien's heroism and social criticism over his earlier "Tale of Turin." Thingol's *ofermod* and Beren's brashness and blind adherence to a flawed social code are answered by the heroic characters Lúthien and Huan whose chief attributes are love and devotion; through them Tolkien begins developing his true heroism. Their loyalty and devotion are represented best in the conquering of the two greatest enemies of Middle-earth: Lúthien enchants Morgoth allowing Beren to steal the Silmaril, and Huan defeats Sauron, causing him to retreat into his spectral form. The main action of the story, however, is still given over to Beren's quest which, acting partially out of love for Lúthien but more so to fulfill a chivalric code, places the pursuit of power, embodied in the Silmarils, at the center of the narrative; Tolkien had yet to define his anti-quest, the relinquishing of power, exemplified in Frodo and Sam's attempt to destroy the Ring of Power. Also, Tolkien's heroics are not yet well defined. Although he has utilized his interpretations of *Gawain's* distinction between flawed social code and higher morality, Tolkien has yet to imbue his heroes with his own ideals, which he would not do until the sub-creation of the Hobbit.

Though Tolkien's *The Hobbit* (1938) has been criticized in comparison with his more developed work, *The Lord of the Rings*, as both overly simplistic and a tale only for children, Tolkien's first published story shows a major advancement of his heroic code and through that the strengthening of his social criticism.[39] In his creation of Bilbo there begins a crystallization of his specific answer to *ofermod,* yet the Hobbit's strength of social criticism is lessened without the religious and moral undertone found more predominantly within the *The Lord of The Rings*. In *The Hobbit*, too, characters of *ofermod* are still presented, but the traditional hero has now been moved to the perimeter of the story, as Tolkien's original sub-creation of the Hobbit becomes the narrative's major concern.

Bilbo Baggins is a rather reluctant hero, but one completely devoid of *ofermod;* his main concerns are not of a quest for power but rather the simplicity of lifestyle found within his home at Bag End in the Shire. He is content in smoking his pipe, in eating plentifully, and in overall relaxation away from adventures into a wider world, but through his mother, Belladonna Took, there is a distant connection with what is seen in the Shire as the socially unacceptable rowdiness of adventure: "Once in a while members of the Took-clan would go and have adventures. They discreetly disappeared, and the family hushed it up; but the fact remained that the Tooks were not as respectable as the Bagginses, though they were undoubtedly richer" (Hobbit, 3). Still, when Gandalf comes to call on Bilbo to proposition him for adventure in the Wilds beyond the Shire, Bilbo is quick to refuse, saying politely as possible, "Sorry! I don't want any adventures, thank you. Not today. Good morning! But please come to tea – any time you like! Why not tomorrow? Come tomorrow! Good-bye!" (6). Unlike characters of dominating will, however, Bilbo is quickly persuaded to come on the adventure with Gandalf, Thorin, and the twelve other dwarves, to serve as the burglar of the quest.[40]

The quest within *The Hobbit* is traditional, however, involving reclamation of wealth and power, specifically in reinstating Thorin as King Under the Mountain, so this earlier story does not exhibit the heightened moral undertones of the anti-quest of the relinquishing of power exhibited in the *The Lord of The Rings*. In the aspect of the initial and, for the majority of the narrative, sustained action of the story is one of glory for the dwarves, and mirrors Beowulf's motivation in the reclamation of Heorot for Hrothgar. In the context of the quest, however, the Beowulf figure has been replaced, or moved to the perimeter and embodied in characters such as Thorin and Bard, while the thief of the original tale is given centrality in Bilbo. Though the narrative of a traditional quest remains intact, the obtainment of power through wealth or prestige, the heroic adventurer has been replaced by a reluctant and bungling hero. After Thorin suggests they should storm the Front Gate to reclaim his throne from the dragon's horde, Gandalf explains:

> Not without a mighty Warrior, even a Hero. I tried to find one; but warriors are busy fighting one another in distant lands, and in this neighborhood heroes are scarce, or simply not to be found. Swords in these parts are mostly blunt, and axes are used for trees, and shields as cradles or dish-covers; and dragons are comfortably far off... That is why I settled on burglary – (21)

The majority of the quest within *The Hobbit* involves episodic monster encounters and serves to develop Bilbo's simplistic character development, punctuated with chapters of respite in loci of social space found in The Last Homely Home, the aerie of the eagles, and Beorn's cabin. The monster encounters, however, are not connected; each monster is acting of his own accord instead of for some malign plans of some dark lord pitted against the sacred morality of the realm. This is a particular weakness of this early story involving hobbits, for just as the monster's strength is weakened so is the urgency and depth of the hero's actions. Similarly, Bilbo's actions are given to less moral depth, so that, initially, his actions are more self serving than in service for some greater good. Paul H. Kotcher writes in *Master of Middle-Earth*:

> Bilbo's enemies are serial, not united under any paragon of evil, as is to happen in the epic. *The Hobbit*'s trolls, goblins (orcs), spiders, and dragon know nothing of one another and are acting on their own. They are certainly not shown to be servants of the nameless and nebulous Necromancer (31).

Thus *The Hobbit* illustrates that the heroics of a quest narrative, and the overall depth of the story, depend upon the greatness of monsters. The stronger and more related of will the monsters, the deeper the moral emphasis and importance for the victory of the hero. In his children's story, Tolkien has yet to give his narrative the moral depth necessary for his sub-creation to reflect adequately the religiousness he saw inherent in the Primary world. Bilbo's quest, then, is necessarily, at first, one of personal gain, specifically material gain, and only near the conclusion of the narrative does Bilbo gain moral insight. Asks Bilbo of the quest: "What am I going to get out of it? And am I going to come back alive?"

It should be said as well that the male bond between Bilbo and the dwarves is particularly weak, Bilbo acting neither through friendship nor servitude, but rather employment, for the dwarves. As such, the dwarves see Bilbo as a tool that can be utilized as they see fit to succeed in the reclamation of their wealth. Speak the dwarves to Bilbo during their first monster encounter involving the three trolls, William, Bert, and Tom: "'Now it is the burglar's turn,' they said, meaning Bilbo. 'You must go on and find out all about that light, and what it is for, and if all is perfectly safe and canny,' said Thorin to the hobbit. 'Now scuttle off, and come back quick, if all is well. If not, come back if you can!'" (34).

Connected to this lack of male friendship is the lack of servitude both to a mortal lord and to a lord infinite. In *The Fellowship of the Ring*, the members of the fellowship form bonds between each other out of recognition that they are working against a great evil and toward a just end to the war beginning in Middle-earth. Sam acts out of loyalty to Frodo, and Frodo out of loyalty to Gandalf, Bilbo, and Elrond. Gimli and Legolas form a friendship which contradicts the feud between their two races. In Bilbo's situation there are no such bonds since there is little moral depth to the tale (until the final chapters and Bilbo's sacrifice of the Arkenstone) in comparison to *The Lord of The Rings*, but also because Bilbo is taken out of his element and no other hobbits journey with him on the quest. Within *The Hobbit*, it should be said that the twelve dwarves with Thorin are acting in his service and are loyal to him, but Thorin, as it turns out, is guilty of *ofermod*, which results in the deaths of two of his loyal followers. Also, in truth, the bond between Thorin and his dwarves is not developed but simply given within the story of *The Hobbit*.

Not until Bilbo's encounter with Smaug and the ensuing actions of Bilbo does *The Hobbit* truly begin to exhibit Tolkien's fully developed heroic æsthetic. What first needs mention is the character of Bilbo's interaction with Smaug: it is particularly not like Beowulf or Tolkien's earlier tale of Turin in the fact that Bilbo does not die, nor does he slay the dragon; this act is left to Bard from Lake Town. Instead, it is Thorin who is eventually destroyed through his reclamation of the dragon's horde and the following Battle of Five Armies. After Smaug is dead, Thorin takes up the space of the monster. Through Bilbo's theft of the cup, and Bard's Black Arrow, Smaug is smitten, and Thorin, like Hrothgar, is left to reclaim his kingdom, but the dwarves' wealth is intermingled with the wealth of other nations which Smaug has hoarded together. Thorin, though, would keep the entirety of wealth for himself, even though it was Bard's valiant actions which brought doom to the evil *wyrm*. Thorin's greediness mirrors Smaug's, so that he becomes the monster of the narrative, and that is why *The Hobbit* does not end with the dragon slaying but with Thorin's and the reclamation of the hoard by Bard to do social good:

> 'Farewell, good thief,' he said. 'I go now to the halls of waiting to sit beside my fathers, until the world is renewed. Since I leave now all gold and silver, and go where it is of little worth, I wish to part in friendship from you, and I would take back my words and deeds at the Gate' (288).

In his dying words, Thorin redeems himself, though his *ofermod* has wrought his doom.[41]

In the character of Bard, Tolkien gives answer to Thorin's *ofermod;* Bard is a just ruler of men who distributes wealth and power for the good of his people. Bard, as a typical heroic leader, however, has been removed from the central narrative of Tolkien's story. His actions of heroism operate on the perimeter, occurring on the story's outskirts, similar to the Beowulf poet's thief in that story; it seems that Tolkien has switched the focus of his story, removing the just heroes to the outskirts of his story, yet he still utilizes Bard at a crucial moment in the narrative. Bard, not guilty of *ofermod*, is not killed by Smaug nor the ensuing battle and he is left to rule justly over his people; but it is specifically Bilbo's sacrifice of the Arkenstone which allows for Bard's instatement over the people. Here, near the end of the narrative, Bilbo finds service under the good leader, Bard, though the relationship between the two is sketchy at best, and not focused upon within the narrative. It must be seen, however, that Bard is a just ruler, and his acquisition and proper distribution of Smaug's horde is made possible through Bilbo's "betrayal" of a corrupt lord:

> From that treasure Bard sent much gold to the Master of Laketown; and he rewarded his followers and friends freely. To the Elvenking he gave the emeralds of Girion, such jewels as he most loved, with which Dain had restored to him.
> To Bilbo he said: 'This treasure is as much yours as it is mine; though old agreements cannot stand, since so many have a claim in its winning and defence. Yet even though you were willing to lay aside all your claim, I should wish that the words of Thorin, of which he repented, should not prove true: that we should give you little. I would reward you most richly of all. (291)

Bilbo is a very different character by the time he and the dwarves reach the Misty Mountains, and he has nearly reached the apex of his character development. Bilbo, through the course of the adventure, has saved the dwarves a multitude of times after Gandalf left them at the edge of Mirkwood. He saves them first from the spiders in Mirkwood and then devises a plan to free the dwarves from the bondage of the wood elves. Bilbo's courage may be said to be represented through his finding of the ring, Gollum's birthday present, and his besting of Gollum through the riddle game. By the time they have reached the secret door to

Smaug's horde, Bilbo is confident in himself, but he has yet to find a true purpose in his quest. He goes alone to search out Smaug's horde, and only Balin of the dwarves goes halfway with him before returning. At this point of the story, Bilbo is in danger of becoming too bold, as the bragging game with Smaug attests: "'I am the friend of bears and the guest of eagles. I am Ringwinner and Luckwearer; and I am Barrel-rider,' went on Bilbo beginning to be pleased with his riddling" (221). And when he sees the glorious jewel, the Arkenstone, he wishes it for himself and hoards it secretly from Thorin:

> It was the Arkenstone, the Heart of the Mountain. So Bilbo guessed from Thorin's description; but indeed there could not be two such gems, even in so marvelous a hoard, even in all the world. Ever as he climbed, the same white gleam had shone before him and drawn his feet towards it. Slowly it grew to a little globe of pallid light. Now as he came near, it was tinged with a flickering sparkle of many colours at the surface, reflected and splintered from the wavering light of his torch. At last he looked down upon it, and he caught his breath. The great jewel shone before his feet of its own inner light, and yet, cut and fashioned by the dwarves, who had dug it from the heart of the mountain long ago, it took all light that fell upon it and changed it into ten thousand sparks of white radiance shot with glints of the rainbow.
> Suddenly, Bilbo's arm went towards it drawn by its enchantment. His small hand would not close about it, for it was a large and heavy gem; but he lifted it, shut his eyes, and put it in his deepest pocket (235).

Reminiscent of the Silmarils, the Arkenstone tests Bilbo's possessiveness, but unlike Fëanor,[42] when Bilbo is confronted with the situation of Thorin's greed, he is able to give up the power and wealth the jewel represents for the greater social good. Knowing the importance Thorin places on the Arkenstone, Bilbo hopes that in his handing over of the jewel to Bard and Gandalf (who serves as a moral compass for Bilbo) he will end the siege upon Thorin and the dwarves. Such altruistic gift-giving is echoed by Bilbo in the opening act of the *The Lord of The Rings*, as he leaves the One Ring behind, and acts as a harbinger for the larger tale of the destruction of the Ring by Frodo in the depths of Mount Doom. Even though Bilbo's use of the

Arkenstone to broach peace results on Thorin's declaration of Bilbo's treacherousness, Bilbo's actions place him away from the *ofermod* of Smaug and Thorin, and in the realm of Huan and Gawain, who are able to dismiss social coding for a higher moral order.

The Hobbit is of critical importance to Tolkien's social criticism because with the creation of Bilbo, Tolkien finally begins to give a solid answer to Anglo-Saxon *ofermod*, instead of simply mirroring the technique of subtle criticism upon a overbold leader of the people. Tolkien's heroic answer is in its infancy here, and only begins to develop within the last few chapters of *The Hobbit*; the rest of the narrative is occupied with disconnected monster encounters punctuated with respite within loci of tamed wilderness. Tolkien's heroic æsthetics of nature, male friendship, and religious undertoning can be found in the narrative, but are underdeveloped and rather insignificant to the plot. Perhaps the most important purpose of *The Hobbit*, as recognized by Kotch, is that it served to introduce the Ring (though gave the talisman of power no deeper moral conception), and serves to introduce Tolkien to a sub-created world and race, the Hobbit, which would mould into a deeper and more socially relevant story within the *The Lord of The Rings*.

6

A MORAL CONCLUSION

Tolkien's social criticism culminates in his most popular work, *The Lord of The Rings*. This tale of moral and religious strife set upon the backdrop of the turmoil of Middle-earth positioned Tolkien's views upon an Industrial Age which made men into machines, and placed society further and further away from nature, while isolating the individual in technology, telling him all the time that there was no god. Tolkien reacts from personal strife: the death of his mother and father while he was still young, his loss of friends in the First World War, and the perils put upon his son Christopher in the Second. In *The Lord of The Rings*, Tolkien finally gives a distinguishably well-developed answer to the *ofermod* in *The Battle of Maldon*, and the *ofermod* of his time which threatened to destroy the world.

The advancement of the *The Lord of The Rings* over *The Hobbit* are the advancements in the larger purpose and significance of Bilbo's magic ring. In the original story, the ring is but a magical toy with no larger significance than an aid for Bilbo's character development, but in *The Lord of The Rings* the One Ring is the symbol of ultimate power, dangerous and world-consuming power which, if wielded by a ruler through *ofermod*, will destroy the earth. Even more so, the Ring symbolizes the corrupted power of an Industrialized Age; Sauron's spirit is within the Ring and his will to dominate Middle-earth. The Ring has been compared to the creation of atomic weaponry, and in the destruction of the Ring is Tolkien's rejection of Modernity and desire to a return to a simpler, more agrarian society. The carrying of the Ring toward destruction, the destruction of riches and power, is Tolkien's anti-quest (as Sam and Frodo are his anti-heroes when associated with Anglo-Saxon heroes who follow a heroic or chivalric code of honor). The forsaking of the Ring's power is in specific counteraction to Tolkien's interpretation of *ofermod*, and the act of laying oneself penitent before a higher moral order. The Ring is the binding symbol of what Tolkien rejects through the *The Lord of The Rings*, and the casting of the fey talisman into the fiery mouth of Mount Doom is Tolkien's ultimate rejection of absolute power wielded by man.

Significantly, Frodo and Sam do not die in the final actions of the narrative, as they are saved by Gandalf and the eagles (just as significantly, Boromir dies from Orc arrows at the beginning of *The Two Towers*); if they had exhibited typical Anglo-Saxon heroics then death by all-powerful monsters would most likely have been their fate—and was almost Frodo's when he refused to give up the Ring only to be set upon by Gollum. Instead, because they serve a higher moral order and do not exhibit *ofermod*, like Gawain they are spared. Gollum, the complicated monster, unwittingly sacrifices himself for the two hobbits; he, a distant and corrupted relation, is the perfect monster in the regard that he represents, like Grendel, the precarious moral path which men must tread. Importantly, humanity can be seen within Gollum, and he may be pitied, but for Tolkien it also must be remembered that ultimately Gollum made a moral decision, like Cane, and has fallen because of it: he is a warning for all humanity, for humans, as well, are distant relations to hobbits, and they too are capable of moral corruption.

In the character of Sam Gamgee Tolkien's heroism is most fully developed. Sam is a gardener and is gifted with the germinating earth which restores the Shire after Saruman has destroyed it. Sam also shares an undying bond with Frodo, a bond both of friendship and fidelity. In this regard, he is the further development of the heroic layering seen in the Tale of Beren: he is a servant of a servant, and thus is even more heroic than Frodo. Sam is aware of a deeper layering to the story, a deeper moral and religious truth, but he is content in the end with a simple life which does not try to delve harmfully into the knowledge of the world. He will marry Rosie Cotton and start a family with her, and he is left on Middle-earth, in faithful servitude of it, while Frodo, tainted and sickened by the Ring, travels with Gandalf and the elves to the far West, where the Valar still reside in a land symbolic of death and the afterlife. Given Sam's significance as the full development of Tolkien's hero, an unassuming man who is faithful above all things, it is not surprising that the story begun by Bilbo and picked up by Frodo is left by Frodo for Sam: "'I have quite finished, Sam,' said Frodo. 'The last pages are for you'" (RK, 380).

The Lord of The Rings's adherence to Tolkien's heroic æsthetic has already been outlined in Chapter Three of this study. What must be concluded is that Tolkien, either knowingly or unwittingly, was cultivating his social criticism through the process of his work. The early versions of the Tales of Beren and Turin are less socially significant than the versions found in *The Silmarillion,* and for the most part in these early tales Tolkien is simply creating characters of *ofermod* who, like their Anglo-Saxon counterparts (Beorhtnoth and Beowulf, as Tolkien interprets them), are subtly (or not so subtly as is the case with Turin and Fëanor) criticized for their jeopardizing of the welfare of the people dependent upon them. In Tolkien's observations on *Sir Gawain and the Green Knight*, Tolkien sees social criticism in the centrality of the servant figure and Gawain's ability to place morality above his chivalric code, and Tolkien would apply his interpretation of this poem to his own work; he would cultivate his own servant figure, his Hobbit, and imbue that character with his heroic æsthetic: a closeness to nature, close bonds with other male characters, and an adherence to a higher order, and in that strong religious undertones. Tolkien would take the centrality of the servant a step further and add a layering to his reluctant heroes, so that there are servants to servants, as is the case with Sam, and necessarily within the context of Tolkien's heroic æsthetic those characters who are the most servile are also the most heroic.

It is well known that Tolkien despised critical analysis of his own work, and surely this study would not be an exception. In literary examination, Tolkien saw a destruction of the analyzed work, which only resulted in a bastardized interpretation far from what the author had in mind. Tolkien was first and foremost a philologist, and probably would not admit to being a literary critic, though his essays on *The Battle of Maldon* and *Sir Gawain and the Green Knight* among many others suggest otherwise; but through the focus upon Tolkien's literary criticism, this study has tried to honor Tolkien by interpreting his work as socially significant. Too often the realm of faerie, be it modern stories based in some way upon Tolkien's master work, children's stories new or old, or even the poems of the Anglo-Saxons, are seen as socially irrelevant, escapist, and necessarily nonimportant. Such sentiment echoes Perish and the society represented in Tolkien's allegorical short story, *Leaf by Niggle*, placing social functionality above artistic sub-creation. Artistic sub-creation, though, both reflects upon and re-creates our social code and ideology; Tolkien's literature has added indefinably to this Primary world, but ultimately he was a man in a dying age "looking [forward] into the pit." His work is an *ubi sunt* for the past and a cry against the rise of the machines.

> *Where now the horse and rider? Where is the horn that was blowing?*
> *Where is the helm and the hauberk, and the bright hair flowing?*

Where is the hand on the harpstring, and the red fire glowing?
They have passed like rain on the mountain, like a wind in the
Meadow;
The days have gone down in the West behind the hills into shadow.
Who shall gather the smoke of the dead wood burning,
Or behold the flowing years from the Sea returning?

APPENDIX

Tom Bombadil: Tolkien's Nature Personified

Tom Bombadil is the character from *The Fellowship of the Ring* who best exemplifies the powerful force of nature in *The Lord of The Rings*. Like Tolkien's creation of the Hobbit, Tom Bombadil owes his origins to a series of stories Tolkien made up for his children, but develops into a much more powerful figure as Tolkien's social critique intensified. Tom's origin, then, like Bilbo's, exemplifies both Tolkien's indebtedness to the tradition of children's folklore and Tolkien's developing critical voice. Tolkien's reflections on nature and the destruction of the natural world begin then in the whimsicalness of a child's fairy story which is later introduced into a world of moral and social strife, and in this manner Tom Bombadil undergoes a minor *bildungsroman* as Tolkien's critique of man's abuse of the natural world intensifies. Tolkien's poems on Tom Bombadil were published in the children's book *The Adventures of Tom Bombadil*. An excerpt from the opening poem reads:

> Old Tom Bombadil was a merry fellow;
> bright blue his jacket was and his boots were yellow,
> green were his girdle and his breeches all of leather;
> he wore in his tall hat a swan-wing feather.

> He lived up under Hill, where the Withywindle
> Ran from a grassy well down into the dingle.43 (11)

In the *The Lord of The Rings*, however, Tom, like Tolkien's Hobbit, has undergone a powerful transformation. No longer simply a character from a children's fairy-tale, Tom's presence is that of a nature uncontrollable and unknowable. He is the very power which Tolkien believes man can never understand nor should try to control. Writes Tolkien of Tom, "[he] knew the darkness under the stars when it was fearless—before the Dark Lord came from Outside" (*The Lord of The Rings,* 129). T.A. Shipley describes Tom as a *lusus naturae,* "a one-member category" (80), and though this may be the case, in the context of Tolkien's social criticism, Tom may best be considered as the voice of nature, a pure, powerful being privy to a divine moral ordering with the ability to reflect upon man's flawed social system. Writes Tolkien:

> Tom's words laid bare the hearts of trees and their thoughts, which were often dark and strange, and filled with a hatred of things that go free upon the earth, gnawing, biting, breaking, hacking, burning: destroyers and usurpers. It was not called the Old Forest without reason, for it was indeed ancient... filled with pride and rooted wisdom, and with malice. (FR, 179)

Tom Bombadil is at his most powerful then when Tolkien's social criticism has reached it full fruition in the *The Lord of The Rings*, and his character serves to illustrate a purpose of this study: that Tolkien was a developing social critic who utilized his scholarly study to strengthen his fiction work, and that Tolkien's work was at its best when his social criticism was at its strongest.

Tolkien's Heroic Women

Although often the few female characters in Tolkien's sub-creation simply mirror the role of female domesticity of Tolkien's time or the Victorian Age to which Tolkien wished nostalgically to return, as is the case with Tom Bombadil's Goldberry and Sam's Rossie Cotton, there are several significant exceptions to this rule which deserve mentioning, and may help to redeem Tolkien's seeming lack of social reflection in the case of the female's role within society. The first and most obvious of these characters is Éowyn of Rohan. Although when she first appears in *The Two Towers* she serves the traditional Anglo-Saxon role of cupbearer for Aragorn (similar to Wealhtheow in *Beowulf*), in *The Return of the King* she disobeys her lord Théoden and, under the disguise of the warrior Dernhelm, travels with the Riders of Rohan to Gondor to do battle against the hosts of Mordor. During the heat of battle, Théoden is attacked by the lord of the Nazgul who rides upon a giant bird-like beast, reminiscent of the fossil of some prehistoric pterodactyl. Éowyn, with Merry, charges to her lord's rescue and confronts the Nazgul who warns her not to interfere with him and his prey:

> Come not between the Nazgul and his prey! Or he will not slay thee in the turn. He will bear thee away to the houses of lamentation beyond all darkness, where thy flesh shall be devoured and thy shriveling mind be left naked to the Lidless Eye. (RK, 141)

Éowyn responds: 'But no living man am I! You look upon a woman. Éowyn I am, Éomund's daughter. You stand between me and my lord and kin. Begone, if you be not deathless for living or dark undead, I will smite you, if you touch him' (RK, 141). Éowyn succeeds in her threat, first cutting the head of the Nazgul's mount, then, after Merry has stabbed the Nazgul from behind, Éowyn "with her last strength... drove her sword between mantle and crown, as the great shoulders bowed before her" (RK, 143). In her heroic actions to defend her lord, Éowyn ultimately takes on the role of Tolkien's hero of unquestioning servitude, but her example remains somewhat of an anomaly, for, though her undying service to Théoden corresponds with Tolkien's heroic æsthetic, her sex is only rarely given such a glorified status in Tolkien's world. It may be mentioned now, however, that Éowyn's heroism echoes the earlier heroisms of Lúthien in the Tale of Beren.

Another example of a heroic female is mentioned briefly in Tolkien's *The Silmarillion* in the character of Haleth, a lady warrior who leads her people, the Haladin, during fierce Orc-raids: "[The Haladin] took Haleth for their leader; and she led them at last to Estolad, and there dwelt for a time" (Sil, 146), but Haleth's heroic character is not so simple, for within her is also embodied the excess of *ofermod*: "Haleth desired to move westward again; and though most of her people were against this counsel, she led them forth once more; and they went without help or guidance of the Eldar...and Haleth only brought her people through [the land] with hardship and loss, constraining them to go forward by the strength of her will" (Sil, 146). Though she does not bring her people to utter ruin, Tolkien's language suggests that Haleth's pride caused a great loss to her people. Unlike Éowyn, Haleth, a minor character amid mention of many other minor characters in *The Silmarillion,* serves as an example of a female ruler who may have behaved too brashly, exhibiting Anglo-Saxon *ofermod*.

Some mention should be made of Tolkien's interesting remarks on dwarfwomen which are found in Appendix A to *The Lord of The Rings*. Tolkien's remarks are interesting because within this race of people there seems to be little difference in the roles and appearances of the two sexes, which, like the two examples above, serve as some counteraction for Tolkien's relative lack of social criticism concern the role of women. Writes Tolkien in the concluding section of Appendix A, *Durin's Folk*:

Dis was the daughter of Thrain II. She is the only dwarf-woman named in these histories. It was said by Gimli that there are few dwarf-women, probably no more than a third of the whole people. They seldom walk abroad except at great need. They are in voice and appearance, and in garb if they must go on a journey, so like the dwarf-men that the eyes and ears of other peoples cannot tell them apart. This has given rise to the foolish opinion among Men that there are no dwarf-women, and that the Dwarves 'grow out of stone' (RK, 449).

Tolkien's Religious Allegory: Leaf By Niggle

Niggle is a painter but lives in a society which does not appreciate artistic creation; it is a very practical society emphasizing values which seem to have immediate relevance to the welfare of the social system. While Niggle strives to create a painting centered on a tree with a beautiful landscape surrounding it, he is harangued by the Inspector of Houses who comes to punish Niggle for not helping his neighbor, Parish, fix the roof of Parish's damaged house:

> 'There has been a flood in the valley, and many families are homeless. You should have helped your neighbor to make temporary repairs and prevent the damage from getting more costly to men than necessary. That is the law. There is plenty of material here: canvas, wood, waterproof paint' (106).

The Inspector is referring to Niggle's painting which Niggle has put so much effort and self into; the painting is Niggle's sub-creation, a glimpse of some greater vision Niggle is trying to bring into the primary world, but the Inspector places practicality above art: "'My picture!' exclaimed Niggle. / 'I dare say it is,' said the Inspector. 'But houses come first. That is the law'" (107). Niggle is forced to give up his painting and is taken away by The Driver on a long journey to the Workhouse, a place Niggle is expected to work in for an allotted time to contribute to society, but Niggle faints into darkness at the railroad station. While in this state, which may be representative of death, Niggle is confronted by two voices, the First Voice and the Second Voice, who revue Niggle's endeavors in the world and ultimately agree that a "little gentle treatment" is in order for Niggle.

Awaking, Niggle goes to the railroad station expecting to return home, but instead ends up in a countryside identical to his painting; he has been gifted by his secondary-creation being brought into the primary world:

> He went on looking at the tree. All the leaves he had ever laboured at were there, as he had imagined them rather than as he had made them; and there were others that had only budded in his mind, and many that might have budded, if only he had had time. Nothing was written on them, they were just exquisite leaves, yet they were dated as clear as a calendar. Some of the most beautiful - and the most characteristic, the most perfect examples of Niggle style - were seen to have been produced in collaboration with Mr. Parish: there was no other way of putting it.
> The birds were building in the Tree. Astonishing birds: how they sang! They were mating, hatching, growing wings, and flying away singing into the Forest, even while he looked at them. For now he saw that the Forest was there too, opening out on either side, and marching away into the distance. The Mountains were glimmering far away (144).

Niggle's painting is actualized and brought into the primary world by the endeavors of the First and Second Voice, but more importantly the action is representative of the importance Tolkien took in creative endeavor; literature and art were important primarily for Tolkien because they added to the world without trying to manipulate the world, and by creating one attempted to move closer to the Great Creator, God, and thus honored him in the act of secondary-creation. The "gods" of Niggle's story, the First and Second voices recognize the importance of Niggle's creation and incorporate it into their primary design; they also chastise Perish for blindly conforming to social expectation in his lack of appreciation for Niggle's art:

> 'He tried to tell you long ago,' said the man; 'but you would not look. He had only got canvas and paint in those days, and you wanted to mend your roof with them. This is what you and your wife used to call Niggle's Nonsense, or That Daubling.'...
> '...It was only a glimpse then,' said the man; 'but you might have caught the glimpse, if you had ever thought it worth while to try' (TR, 117).

Eventually Niggle follows a shepherd up to the mountains, because he is "ready to move on," while *Niggle's Parish in the bay* becomes a popular spot for people to visit. *Leaf by Niggle* implies both that the creative act is more important than social functionality and may contribute greatly to society both through artistic vision and social criticism (especially when that act is directed towards a higher moral code), and that secondary-creation can have an everlasting effect upon people, transporting them to a place they are not able to go to within the primary world. Ultimately, Niggle involves himself in a heroic endeavor of creation and does not blindly adhere to the social values around him; Though Niggle is not Tolkien's typical hero, he does serve to show the great importance Tolkien bestowed upon his creative act, as well as the situation of that act in a realm of unspecific religious faith.

A segment of Kullervo's Tale from *The Kalevala* which may be seen as the origins for Turin's romance with his sister Nienori:

> And by chance a maiden met him,
> Wearing a tin brooch, and singing,
> Out upon the heaths of Pohja,
> And the borders wide of Lapland...
>
> Kullervo, Kalervo's offspring,
> With the very bluest stockings,
> Thereupon the maiden flattered,
> And he wheedled and caressed her,
> With one hand the horse controlling,
> On the maiden's breast the other
> (Kirby, Runnoxv, 133-136, 179-184)

And when the maiden discovers she is Kullervo's sister:

> Quickly from the sledge she darted,
> And she rushed into the river,
> In the furious foaming cataract,
> And amid the raging whirlpool,
> There she found the death that she sought for,
> There at length did death o'ertake her,
> Found in Tuonela a refuge,
> In the waves she found compassion (259-266)

A Will to Dominate: Fëanor's Kinslaying

In 1914, around the same time *The Kalevala* inspired Tolkien to begin the Tale of Turin, which would be the first of his collective mythology gathered in *The Silmarillion,* Tolkien wrote a seemingly nonsensical poem, "The Voyage of Eärendil, the Evening Star". The original poem read:

> Eärendil sprang up from the Ocean's Cup
> In the gloom of the mid-world's rim;
> From the door of night as a ray of light
> Lept over the twilight brim
> And launching his bark like a silver spark
> From the gold-fading sand
> Down the sunlit breath of day's fiery death
> He sped from Westerland. (Tolkien, 71)

This was the original poem set in the world which would become Tolkien's Middle-earth. By 1917, Tolkien had written "The Fall of Gondolin" and "The Children of Húrin," leading to the deeper development for his plans to create a mythology for England. Inspired by *The Kalevala*, the Elder and Younger Eddas, and other mythologies from Denmark, Germany, and Iceland, Tolkien set to work creating the collection of tales which would form the First and Second Ages of Middle-earth; it is important to remember that in the timeline of his sub-created world, Hobbits would not arrive for thousands of years, in the Third Age, the final age chronicled in Tolkien's writing. Wrote Tolkien on his original purpose for creating Middle-earth:

> Do not laugh! But once upon a time... I had a mind to make a body of more or less connected legend, ranging from the large and cosmogonic to the level of romantic fairy-story – the larger founded on the lesser in contact with the earth, the lesser drawing splendour from the vast backcloths – which I could dedicate simply: to England, to my country. It should possess the tone and quality that I desired, somewhat cool and clear, be redolent of our 'air' (the clime and soil of the North West, meaning Britain and hither parts of Europe...) ... I would draw some of the great tales in fullness and leave many... only

sketched. The cycles should be linked to a majestic whole, and yet leave scope for other minds and hands, wielding paint and music and drama. Absurd (Tolkien 89-90).

Tolkien would come close to finally creating this vision, but would die (in 1973) before the publication of *The Silmarillion*, in 1977. Tolkien's great backcloth of mythology, which gives his *The Lord of The Rings* such great depth and purpose, is complicated to gauge in its social criticism; its primary purpose is not of social criticism but of greater mythological creations. Characters rise and fall in an overwhelming time scale which spans two ages and must be reckoned from the viewpoint of Tolkien's gods. The Tales of Turin and Beren, taken on their own, have major characters which the narrative of their stories focuses upon, and through those characters a social message, but in the grander scale of the entirety of *The Silmarillion*, individuals are dwarfed by the purposes of nations and gods, making it very difficult to find a direction of primary social criticism; but even still, Tolkien is working in the same modes of reflection which directed his criticisms of *The Battle of Maldon* and *Sir Gawain and the Green Knight*, so social criticism can be found when looked for. Certainly, however, *The Silmarillion* as a work of social criticism is a mere ripple compared to the final designs in Tolkien's *The Lord of The Rings*. As works of literary art, however, both works are splendidly crafted, and it can only be surmised that *The Silmarillion* was not so overwhelmingly successful as *The Lord of The Rings* because in his mythological creation Tolkien disregarded modern modes of writing and craft altogether, and instead he honored the modes of literature which he studied as an academic.

For the purpose of our study, it will be necessary only to focus analysis on one individual from *The Silmarillion*, for Tolkien's social criticism within this collective text does not go far beyond the *ofermod* exhibited by the Noldor elf Fëanor (this necessarily excludes the isolated examples previously given of the Tales of Turin and Beren – those tales having a larger and complicated existence outside *The Silmarillion*), the son of Finwë and Miriel, the king and queen of Tirion. Originally named Curufinwe, his mother called him Fëanor, Spirit of Fire, and through his possessive and selfish actions the downfall of the Noldor, an entire race of people, would be crafted. The initial curse which Fëanor causes to fall upon the Noldor carries through the entirely of *The Silmarillion*. As the initiator of tragedy among the elves, particularly in the Kinslaying at Alqualonde, Fëanor receives greater character development than is seen in most of the participants in *The Silmarillion*. Recognizing this, Paul H. Kocher, in his work *A Reader's Guide to The Silmarillion*, writes:

> Fëanor, the mightiest genius ever produced by the Elvish race, has a character more complex than that of any other person, be he Elf, Man, or Dwarf, who takes part in the war against Morgoth. Tolkien studies him carefully from many sides, for Fëanor while alive is the mainspring of the disasters that ensue. And after his death his influence is perpetrated by his seven sons, who have sworn to pursue and kill anyone who withholds from them even a single one of the three Silmarils made by their father. So the voice of Fëanor, long dead, may be said to echo down the tragedy to the very end (50).

Even in birth, Fëanor consumes the power of others, for he uses all of Miriel's life energy and she dies soon after. "In the bearing of her son Miriel was consumed in spirit and body: after his birth she yearned for release from the labor of living" (Sil, 63). Speaks Miriel after Fëanor is born, "Never again shall I bear child; for strength that would have nourished the life of many has gone forth into Fëanor" (63). Fëanor grows quickly and is consumed by a quest of self empowerment through the search for knowledge. His father, Finwë, marries again to Indis of the Vanyar Elves and bears Fëanor two half brothers, Fingolfin and Finarfin; but Fëanor is jealous ("envy was in his heart") of the marriage and the birth of his two brothers only serves to make him more withdrawn into his endeavors for knowledge and power. Fëanor, working through magical and pseudoscientific craft, creates the seven seeing stones, the palantír, used afterwards by Sauron and Saruman in the *The Lord of The Rings*. He creates also three stones of great power and light, the Silmarils, of the deeds of elves the closest to mirroring Ilúvatar's creation of life, but Fëanor grows suspicious and hordes, like Tolkien's dragons, the Silmarils for his own.44

Tolkien hints that Fëanor, in his greatness of will, has some foreknowledge of terrible events that are about to fall upon the Valar. Even Mandos, keeper of the House of the Dead in the far West, "foretold that the fates of Arda, earth, sea, and air, lay locked" within the Silmarils. In fact, it is Morgoth's plan to recruit the light devouring she-spider Ungoliant to devour the light of the two life giving trees planted by Yavanna. Fëanor's great creation must be seen as fated through the higher ordering of Ilúvatar who hoped to use Fëanor as an agent against Morgoth, but Fëanor's self-empowering will wishes to possess the power of the Silmarils. Through Fëanor's selfishness and monstrous greed, the power of the Silmarils are left stagnant:

> Fëanor would wear them, blazing on his brow, at other times they were guarded close, locked in the deep chambers of his hoard in Tirion. For Fëanor began to love the Silmarils with a greedy love, and grudged the sight of them to all save to his father and his seven sons; he seldom remembered now that the light within them was not his own. (69)

The rift between Fëanor and his father grows, and during this time Melkor, lusting after the Silmarils, comes to Fëanor and tells him of Ilúvatar's creation of Men in the east (which had been kept secret by Manwë), causing suspicion to grow among the Noldor elves that Manwë might be holding them captive to allow Men the reign of Middle-earth. Melkor plants the lie that Fingolfin is plotting against his brother Fëanor and causes the feud to deepen between the brothers, so that Fëanor openly threatens Fingolfin by drawing his sword against him. Fëanor is banished for twelve years from Tirion (Kocher, 57). In secret with his seven sons, Fëanor begins a construction of a mighty fortress and armament in the north where he broods against his half brothers and hordes his wealth.[45] While Fëanor is banished, Melkor plots to destroy the light of the two Trees, and calls forth Ungoliant, a light-destroying spider and mother to Shelob, from the shadows. Even as a forced truce is made between Fëanor and Fingolfin at a festival before the great Trees, Melkor and Ungoliant strike, destroying the divine trees which bloom day and night into the world.[46]

Encapsulated in Fëanor's Silmarils is the light which may restore life into the Trees and light again upon the Valar and Middle-earth; here is the purpose which Fëanor saw for the creation of his jewels, and which was predicted by Mandos. Yavanna requests that she receive the Silmarils from Fëanor for if she had even a little of their light she would be able to "recall life to the Trees," but Fëanor through his greed and the corruption of Melkor, mistrusts the Valar and he hesitates in reply to Yavanna, but his ultimate answer is one of greed, as he refuses Yavanna's request. Writes Kotch on Fëanor's actions, "His answer was a veiled refusal coupled with an insult. He would not give up the Silmarils of his own free will, he said, and if the Valar forced him to, they would be acting like Morgoth" (60). In his actions, Fëanor fails his people and the Elves of the Teleri and the Vanya; as a leader of men he has too much pride and his greed for the Silmarils mirrors the uselessness of monster hordes.

After Melkor has destroyed the great trees, he rushes through the ensuing darkness to Fëanor's stronghold at Formenos and there slays Fëanor's father, Finwë, and steals away the Silmarils. Enraged, Fëanor curses Melkor and names him "Morgoth, the Black Foe of the World; and by that name only was he known to the Eldar ever after" (79). In his anger, Fëanor goes against Manwë's orders not to leave the Valar, and he swears a terrible and unbreakable oath with his seven sons to travel to Middle-earth and to attack Morgoth where he has built a stronghold in the north called Angband.[47] The dire oath is the initiating action of the downfall of the Noldor, and especially the line of Fëanor, for in the act they raise up this social agreement amongst themselves over a higher ordering, the law and command of the Valar. Fëanor will now sacrifice anything for the reclamation of his Silmarils, and through their bond with their father, Fëanor's children share in his *ofermod*, spreading it through the generations of the Noldor. They uphold the reclamation of power represented in the Silmarils above all else, including the safety and welfare of their people. Writes Kotch upon Fëanor's oath, "Fëanor's Oath sets no limit to the means used in keeping it. So the attempt to keeps it leads his sons from one horrible killing to another, and eventually to Maedros' despairing suicide and Maglor's self-exile from his own kind" (64).

Soon after the declaration of this oath, Fëanor and the majority of the Noldor who chose to follow him, even after Manwë cautions them against it, head eastward in self imposed exile from the Valar. At the western boundary of the Great Sea they petition Olwe, the prince of the Teleri, for the use of the Teleri elves' great fleet of ships to sail to Middle-earth; but Olwe refuses, using Fëanor's own selfishness in the giving of the Silmarils against him, saying that like Fëanor's jewels the Teleri ships were "'the work of our hearts, whose like we shall not make again'" (86). But Fëanor is bound upon his quest by an unbreakable oath and will not be stopped; he wrathfully takes the ships by force, causing the Kinslaying of Alqualonde in which many Teleri are killed and the Noldor with Fëanor are cursed.[48] Fëanor's *ofermod* and through that his Kinslaying has led those Noldor who have taken him as their leader to doom and destruction, not only for themselves but for the generations which will come after them. Fëanor's failure as a leader is an ultimate one and of the highest *ofermod*. Similar to Turin, Fëanor's actions are emblematic of *ofermod* to the extreme.

Fëanor's final act of *ofermod*, which like Beowulf and Beorhtnoth, brings about his own death through brash actions on the battlefield, happens after the Noldor have passed the icefields of Helcaraxë and into Middle-earth. Morgoth, learning of Fëanor's arrival, sends his forces against the Noldor but the elves, though greatly outnumbered, turn the enemy to flight and then head for Angband to destroy Morgoth and reclaim the Silmarils. Fëanor, though, through reckless disregard of himself, and in an altered state brought about by the nearness of the Silmarils and the doom spoken to him from Manwë through Mandros, does not heed his fellow Noldor, and brashly rushes into battle before the other Noldor can gather to him.[49] Though the Noldor are not left to perish after Fëanor's death, for his seven sons take up lordship of those Noldor, there is a greater doom awaiting them: the slow punishment and death wrought by Fëanor's Kinslaying. Fëanor's brashness and will for power corrupted not only destroys himself but also slowly poisons those elves who followed him as their leader. In his character, Tolkien mirrors the Anglo-Saxon *ofermod* of over-bold leaders, but even more than Turin's actions, Fëanor serves as the ultimate example of the results of a social system determined by the actions of one man, if that one man is unjust and power hungry. Like Beowulf, Fëanor's death at the hands of the Lord of the Balrogs comes as the result of a quest for too much power, the monster representative of untamable power, and the inevitable death of the man who tries to wield such power. As Fëanor dies, he holds his sons to their oath and they swear themselves to it once more. Tolkien concludes on Fëanor:

> Then he died; but he had neither burial nor tomb, for so fiery was his spirit that as it sped from his body fell to ash, and was borne away like smoke; and his likeness has never again appeared in Arda, neither has his spirit left the halls of Mandos. Thus ended the mightiest of the Noldor, of whose deeds came both their greatest renown and their most grievous woe. (107)

Fëanor then must be seen as representing the contradiction to Tolkien's true hero, the subservient found at the borders of Anglo-Saxon poetry (and sometimes at the center as in *The Seafarer* and *The Wanderer*). Tolkien, however, had yet to find the person or race which would best embody his true heroism and in the overall mythology of *The Silmarillion* there remains little social criticism beyond a simple reflection of a leader's *ofermod*.

BIOGRAPHICAL SKETCH OF J.R.R. TOLKIEN

John Ronald Reuel Tolkien was born in Bloemfontein, South Africa (then called the Orange Free State) in 1892. In 1895, Tolkien's mother returned with him and his brother to England. In 1896, Tolkien's father died while still in South Africa, and soon after, in 1896, Tolkien's mother died (in 1904). In 1911, Tolkien won a scholarship to Oxford University and afterwards entered the army. In 1916, Tolkien married his wife, Edith Bratt. While in war, Tolkien served in the Battle of Somme, but afterwards was invalided out of the army. In 1917, Tolkien's first son, John was born, and Tolkien began to work on his collective mythology for England, what would become known as *The Silmarillion*. In 1918, Tolkien joined the staff of the *Oxford English Dictionary*, and in 1920 he was appointed Reader in English Language at Leeds University. Soon afterward, his second son, Michael, was born. In 1924, Tolkien's third son, Christopher, was born. In 1925, Tolkien published an edition of *Sir Gawain and the Green Knight* with E.V. Gordon, and he was named Rawlinson and Bosworth Professor of Anglo-Saxon at Oxford University. In 1929, Tolkien's daughter, Priscilla, was born. In 1936, Tolkien gave his famous lecture on Beowulf, "The Monsters and the Critics." In

1937, Tolkien published *The Hobbit*. In 1939, Tolkien gave his lecture *On Fairy-Stories* at St. Andrews University. In 1945, Tolkien was named Merton professor of English Language and Literature at Oxford University. In 1949, Tolkien published *Sir Giles of Ham*. In 1954, Tolkien published *The Fellowship of the Ring* and *The Two Towers*. In 1955, *The Return of the King* was published, even though it was originally supposed to be published as one book entitled *The Lord of the Rings*. In 1959, Tolkien retired from Oxford. In 1962, *The Adventures of Tom Bombadil* was published, and in 1964 *Tree and Leaf* was published. In 1967, *Smith of Wotton Major* was published. Tolkien's wife, Edith, died in 1971 and, in 1973, Tolkien died in Bournemouth. In 1976 and 1977, *The Father Christmas Letters* and *The Silmarillion* are published posthumously (Crabbe, vii-viii).

NOTES

1. It should be understood that this study is not primarily interested in a chronological ordering of the development of Tolkien's social criticism. Rather, it satisfies itself by making the crucial connection between the social observations Tolkien makes in *The Battle of Maldon* and *Sir Gawain and the Green Knight* and the development of social criticism into Tolkien's creative writings. The study then continues by observing the development of Tolkien's heroic ideals and the application of that heroism to his creative fiction as a social model in answer to the strife of modernity. There is, however, a loose chronological development observed in the analysis of four of Tolkien's major fictional texts: *Turin Son of Húrin*, *Beren and Lúthien*, *The Hobbit*, and finally *The Lord of The Rings*. Advances in the social criticism Tolkien develops in these four texts will be discussed in chapter five and in the conclusion of this study.

2. Here it must be said as well that in Tolkien's critical interpretations he is specifically interested in the brashness and absolute will of leaders who placed social will above moral will. The heroic and chivalric codes, for Tolkien, are both flawed social ideals. He does not appear interested in the specifics of each code, rather in the general flaws of each and the elevation of a moral ordering above social law. Such an approach allows for Tolkien to remove *ofermod* from its time and place and apply it to later works, such as *Sir Gawain and the Green Knight*, as well as his own society.

3. Here the term sub-created is taken directly from Tolkien's essay *On*

Fairy-Stories. Tolkien viewed his artistic endeavor as honoring and attempting to mirror God's creation of the Primary World, thus a work of art becomes a sub-creation. Tolkien believed that all art must be derived from primary experience but should not be a simple mirroring of that experience. With the term sub-creation, Tolkien hoped for the immediate validation of the importance of his writing and all purposeful writings which might take place in an extracted realm of faerie, and he also emphasized his view of a moralistic ordering to the universe.

4. Examples of such servile heroes include Wiglaf from the *Beowulf* poem, Beorhtwold from *The Battle of Maldon*, and both voyagers from *The Wanderer* and *The Seafarer*. An even more important example is the character of Gawain from *Sir Gawain and the Green Knight* which does not come until the high Middle Ages. Some of these servant figures cannot be said to be specifically heroic in battle, but it will be shown that Tolkien's heroic ideals placed greater stock in penitent service than in the brashness of battle.

5. Though the Victorian is not the subject of this study, the ideals from the Victorian Age which Tolkien took most stock in and carried through to his literary work are those same ideals which may be seen in his hero, the Hobbit. They include homosocial bonds between men, a pastoral respect for nature, and (though this is not entirely true for Tolkien but may be interpreted in his fiction work) a general Deism or acceptance of God without a specified religion.

6. As a sub-creation hobbits are Tolkien's original invention, but it is important to remember Tolkien's own remarks that all sub-creation is a product of observations of the natural, primary world. With this realization, it must also be remembered that *The Hobbit* was originally a children's story involving a rather basic *bildungsroman* of the main character, Bilbo Baggins. In this context, hobbits are simply another form of a children's folklore hero enmeshed in a story alongside the epic heroes of the Anglo-Saxon tradition. It was ingenious of Tolkien to combine the two traditions: first the one of his main focus of professional study, the Anglo-Saxon, and the other the more recent, or at least more recently printed, folklore children's hero of Germanic, French, and British traditions. There are various sources which could be said to have influenced Tolkien's *The Hobbit*. Some sources that should be considered are Andrew Lang's *Fairy Books,* George McDonald's *Princess and the Goblin* and other novels, and Kenneth Grahame's *Wind in the Willows*. The folklore tradition of these

novels inspired Tolkien and provided the original source for Tolkien's Hobbit. Along with his own children's stories created to amuse his children at bedtime, these stories combined with Tolkien's earlier sources, which included *Sir Gawain and the Green Knight, Beowulf,* the *Volsunga Saga*, the *Nibelungenlied*, and the Finnish *Kalevala*. Perhaps, as Deborah Rogers notes in her *Fictitious Characters*, it was the simplistic character growth or *bildungsroman* which attracted Tolkien to the tradition of children's folklore, for as Rogers notes, there is no "growing succession" in *Beowulf*, just initial and final pictures (21). In *The Lord of The Rings* Tolkien would expound upon that basic character growth, and in Frodo create a heroic-saint whose life and actions would serve as a model for Tolkien's age. What should be noted, however, is that, initially, Tolkien is combining two traditions, that of the child's folktale and epic Anglo-Saxon poetry. Tolkien's first literary outing which involves his hobbits is primarily a child's folktale with Anglo-Saxon elements, but in his second effort the character of the Hobbit is changed, given deeper definition and purpose and thrust into a world in chaos, one in which a new type of hero is sorely necessary. Though the Hobbit's origins remain that of the Germanic and British children's folklore tradition, in *The Lord of the Rings* the Hobbit gains a higher moral purpose and heroic mission, and has been imbued thoroughly with Tolkien's æsthetics and moral inclinations.

7. Tolkien's heroic æsthetic will be discussed in much detail in Chapter Three of this study.

8. Joseph Bosworth and T. Northcote Toller in the magisterial *Anglo-Saxon Dictionary* define the noun as 'pride, arrogance, over-confidence' (West, 235).

9. Richard West in his essay, "Turin's Ofermod," writes, "There are many [critics] who argue that this sort of heroic excess was considered highly admirable by the Anglo-Saxons and by other medieval peoples both before and long after the time of the poem. This may be typified by the assertion of Ralph W.V. Elliott that heroes such as Beorhtnoth 'court disaster magnificently, with their eyes wide open, and, according to their lights, rightly'" (236).

10. Tolkien renders lines 89 and 90 of the poem as follows: "then the earl in his overmastering pride actually yielded ground to the enemy, as he should not have done" (TR, 21).

11. And Tolkien interprets *ofermod* as a derogatory term implying the misuse of power by one in power and the resulting social ills of the overboldness of that one's actions.

12. This, of course, was not done directly in a fictionalized modern world but in the space of Middle-earth.

13. In *The Homecoming of Beorhtnoth Beorhthelm's Son* this connection is most explicit. In effect, Tolkien is recreating the Anglo-Saxon poem for modernity. Can it be said that in part Tolkien saw similar failures in the modern social code and wished to utilize the social criticism he understood to be inherent in the Anglo-Saxon term *ofermod* to provide social criticism for his own time? What is for certain is that this play is the clearest link between Tolkien's scholarly study and his artistic endeavors.

14. This, of course, takes for granted views of the poem in opposition to Tolkien who saw the entire poem as an "extended comment on, or illustration of the words of the old retainer Beorhtwold" (TR, 21). Thus, as in Tolkien's play, the retainer reflects upon the problematic impact of an unjust ruler on society.

15. This change does not come to its full fruition until Tolkien's seminal work, *The Lord of The Rings*.

16. This comment relates both to Tolkien's Christianity and his understanding of the Anglo-Saxon world. Like his scholarly and artistic approaches to literature, here is another amalgam of Tolkien's interests which works well together. Tolkien relates the piety and undying faith of the servant figure, his Sam, to both a heavenly and earthly lord, yet Tolkien's heavenly devotion is left nondescript in the land of Middle-earth; this is one of Tolkien's heroic ideals and will be discussed in more detail in Chapter 3 of this study.

17. It can be observed in Tolkien's play by the complete removal (by death) of the traditional heroic figure.

18. Some examples which come readily to mind are: from the Old English heroic epic, Heorot in *Beowulf*; from Middle English romantic literature, Arthur's Camelot in *Sir Gawain and the Green Knight* and the corpus of other writings on Arthur; and from the classical epic, the episodic nature of the *Iliad* and *Odyssey*. In fact, the general form of *The*

Hobbit and *The Lord of The Rings*, like Beowulf, may be said to be derived generally from the Virgilian code of violence, gift giving, and rest.

19. Examples of such power would include atomic weaponry, cloning, and genetic engineering.

20. Further discussion on Tolkien's nature æsthetic can be found in the Appendix in the section discussing the importance of Tom Bombadil.

21. Such male bonds relate directly to the Anglo-Saxon leader and subordinate relationship Tolkien discusses in "Ofermod" (His essay on *The Battle of Maldon* which can be found following *The Homecoming of Beorhtnoth Beorhthelm's Son* in the *Tolkien Reader*.) M.G. London's essay "Lead, Follow, or Go Over the Sea" further analyses how Tolkien applies his understanding of *ofermod* to the male relationships in *The Lord of The Rings* and discusses the proper responsibilities a lord must show his servants.

22. Although, strictly speaking, Wiglaf is not a true servant figure but a "prince of the Scylfings," he still owes his allegiance to his liege-lord, Beowulf. Tolkien never defines the exact nature of Sam's relationship to Frodo other than that Sam is Frodo's gardener and friend. There is no reason for Sam to serve Frodo save for their bond of homosocial friendship; this, perhaps, makes Sam's bond to Frodo even stronger than Wiglaf's bond to Beowulf.

23. A brief analysis of Tolkien's female heroines can be found in the Appendix.

24. Tolkien's approach to *Beowulf* in his essay *The Monsters and the Critics* isn't covered in this study, but would provide support for the claim of Tolkien operating as a social critic, especially concerning the religious ideals in place in his heroic æsthetic. The essay defends the centrality of the monsters in Beowulf as a strengthening of the overall conflict of the poem and the moral danger the hero, Beowulf, is involved in.

25. There is one exception in Tolkien's corpus, however, the short story *Leaf by Niggle* which is an allegory of the importance Tolkien saw within art as sub-creation elevated in social importance above "practical" acts which may appear to have greater social functionality. A brief analysis of this short story, found in the Appendix, will serve to illustrate the

religious purpose Tolkien placed upon his secondary creation of Middle-earth.

26. As with Tolkien's interpretation of *ofermod* in *The Battle of Maldon*, his interpretation of the actions and the purpose of the *Sir Gawain and the Green Knight* poem have been opposed by critics. The purpose of this study, however, is to show Tolkien's social criticism and the relationship of his analysis of *Sir Gawain and the Green Knight* and the development of his own heroic code in his fictional corpus; his critical analysis of *Sir Gawain and the Green Knight* does exactly this and it does not serve the purpose of the study to focus attention on differing interpretations of the poem.

27. Writes Tolkien of Gawain's significance: "His motivation is a humble one: the protection of Arthur, his elder kinsman, of his king, of the head of the Round Table, from indignity and peril, and the risking instead of himself, the least of the knights (as he declares), and the one whose loss could most easily be endured. He is involved therefore in the business, as far as it was possible to make the fairy-story go, as a matter of duty and humility and self-sacrifice" (75).

28. Roger C. Schlobin in his essay, "The Monsters Are Talismans and Transgressions; Tolkien and Sir Gawain and the Green Knight" gives some other possibilities of character connections between *The Lord of The Rings* and *Sir Gawain and the Green Knight* and upholds the comparison of Sam and Gawain: "John F. Fyler draws parallels between Frodo's and Gawain's 'passive endurance', and Miller suggests one between Tom Bombadil and the Green Knight/ Bertilak. Certainly, both Frodo's and Gawain's commitment to their quests demonstrate their comparable endurance. However, Gawain is hardly passive. His aggressiveness is demonstrated by his willingness to stop Arthur from accepting the Green knight's challenge... Samwise [in comparison to Gawain] is probably a better illustration of this resiliency than Frodo since he is not infected by the Ring and is more of a 'pure hobbit.' After the Ring's destruction and Frodo's acceptance of 'the end of things,' it is Samwise who says, 'But after coming all that way I don't want to give up yet. It is not like me, somehow, if you understand' (RK 275) (73).

29. In Frodo's relationship with the Ring, Tolkien's message becomes somewhat complicated. Frodo is given a taste of absolute power and he is sickened and consumed by it, but Frodo must also bear the object of power

to destroy it. With such a relationship, Tolkien may be saying that a position of power must be obtained in order to deconstruct and reshape that power, but such an endeavor creates a Catch-22 situation, for, once tasted, the want for power can not be left behind and inevitably destroys a person.

30. It is interesting to note here that Gawain's quest is a solitary one, while Frodo is a member of a group of nine, one of which, Aragorn, is closely related to Arthur in the fact that he is hero king, and it is particularly interesting that Tolkien would allow Aragorn to involve himself so directly in the actions of the quest, considering the social importance which is put upon Aragorn's welfare. It is also true, however, that Aragorn has removed himself from a position of power, abandoning Gondor to Denethor and the Stewards, and taking solitude and almost monk-like refuge in the north, going by the name Strider; so it is necessary for Aragorn to travel with Frodo back to a space of heroic endeavor if only to reclaim his rightful throne in Gondor. Can it be said that in some sense, Aragorn is following Frodo's lead and takes a lesson from Tolkien's new heroism embodied in Frodo the hobbit?

31. "Gawain meets the good man in the middle of the floor,
And he greeted him graciously, and gleefully he said,
'I shall fulfill at first our fixed covenant now,
That we speedily spoke about when no drink was spared.'
Gawain clasps the knight and gives him three kisses,
As surely and soundly as he could secure them" (1932-1937)

32. This is specifically referring to Wiglaf.

33. "Turambar and the Foaloke" (1919) in *The Book of Lost Tales Part Two*, *The Lay of the Children of Húrin* (1920-25) in *The Lays of Beleriand, Narn I Hin Húrin* "The Tales of the Children of Húrin" (1920s-1930s?) in *Unfinished Tales*, in parts in the other volumes of Christopher Tolkien's *History of Middle-earth* which deal with Tolkien's First Age (*The Shaping of Middle-earth, The Lost Road, Morgoth's Ring*, and *The War of the Jewels*, and finally in summary form in chapter 21 of *The Silmarillion* (West, 240-241).

34. West summarizes: "Untamo, with his retainers, attacks and kills his brother, Kalervo, and all his household save one woman who is pregnant and is apparently spared for that reason. Her son is named Kullervo, and he

is also Kalervo's son... [Kullervo] is eventually sold as a slave to one of the major characters in the Kalevala, Ilmarinen the Smith, but all his work turns out awry as it had when he was labouring for Untamo..., since his heroic strength results in such things as pulling apart fishing nets instead of hauling in fish. While he is traveling by sledge he on three occasions passes women and each time tries to entice them to accept a ride. They all prudently decline, but the third time he forces the young woman into the sledge and then bribes and wheedles her into lying with him. Only afterward do they discover that she is his missing sister, and she immediately drowns herself in remorse for their unwitting incest" (237-238).

35. Húrin is Turin's father, who is forced to watch the unfolding of his son's fate while held captive by Melkor; it is from Húrin's viewpoint that the story is framed, adding greater tragedy to the story.

36. A portion of *The Kalevala* which closely relates to Turin's romance with his sister can be found in the Appendix of this study.

37. In *The Silmarillion* version of the tale, Tevildo has been replaced by Sauron, and there is a deepening of the urgency and extent of Beren's plight through the alignment of the enemy. The strengthening of monsters creates a deepening of the overall jeopardy felt in the story.

38. "This mighty beech was named Hirilorn, and it had three trunks, equal in girth, smooth in rind, and exceedingly tall; no branches grew from them for a great height above the ground. Far aloft between the shafts of Hirilorn a wooden house was built, and there Lúthien was made to dwell; and the ladders were taken away and guarded, save only when the servants of Thingol brought her such things as she needed.
"It is told in the Lay of Leithian how she escaped from the house in Hirilorn; for she put forth her arts of enchantment, and caused her hair to grow to great length, and of it she wove a dark robe that wrapped her beauty like a shadow, and it was laden with a spell of sleep" (Sil, 172).

39. Tolkien's Hobbit is his agent of heroism and serves as a model for modern society to follow.

40. "Then something Tookish woke up inside him, and he wished to go and see the great mountains, and hear the pine-trees and the waterfalls, and explore the caves, and wear a sword instead of a walking-stick. He

looked out of the window. The stars were out in a dark sky above the trees. He thought of the jewels of the dwarves shining in dark caverns. Suddenly in the wood beyond The Water a flame leapt up - probably somebody lighting a wood-fire - and he thought of plundering dragons settling on his quiet Hill and kindling it all to flames. He shuddered; and very quickly he was plain Mr. Baggins of Bag-End, Under-Hill, again" (15).

41. Thorin's actions in the novel can be interpreted as *ofermod* because his brashness for battle with a force much greater than his own places those loyal to him in danger. He is specifically operating as a lord over his dwarven companions and putting them in danger through his recklessness. He is greedy, as well, but it is his over-brashness for battle which relates his actions to Tolkien's interpretation of *ofermod*.

42. Fëanor's *ofermod* is discussed in the final portion of this study's Appendix.

43. In the context of this poem, several other important characters of the opening acts to *The Fellowship of the Ring* occur; these characters include Goldberry, Old Man Willow, and the Barrow-wight.

44. "For Fëanor, being come to his full might, was filled with a new thought, or it may be that some shadow of foreknowledge came to him of the doom that drew near; and he pondered how the light of the Trees, the glory of the Blessed Realm, might be preserved imperishable. Then he began a long, secret labour, and he summoned all his lore, and his power, and his subtle skill; and at the end of all he made the Silmarils.
"As three jewels they were in form... Yet the crystal was to the Silmarils but as is the body to the Children of Ilúvatar: the house of its inner fire, that is within it and yet in all parts of it, and is its life. And the inner fire of the Silmarils Fëanor made of the blended light of the Trees of Valinor, which lives in them yet, though the Trees have long withered and shine no more. Therefore even in the darkness of the deepest treasury the Silmarils of their own radiance shone like the stars of Varda; and yet, as were they indeed living things, they rejoiced in light and received it and gave it back in hues more marvelous that before" (Sil, 67).

45. "With him into banishment went his seven sons, and northward in Valinor they made a strong place and treasury in the hills; and there at Formenos a multitude of gems were laid in hoard, and weapons also, and the Silmarils were shut in a chamber of iron. Thither also came Finwë the

King, because of the love he bore to Fëanor; and Fingolfin ruled the Noldor in Tirion. Thus the lies of Melkor were made true in seeming, though Fëanor by his own deeds had brought this thing to pass; and the bitterness that Melkor had sown endured, and lived still long after between the sons of Fingolfin and Fëanor" (Sil, 71).

46. "Then the Unlight of Ungoliant rose up even to the roots of the Trees, and Melkor sprang upon the mound; and with his black spear he smote each Tree to its core, wounded them deep, and their sap poured forth as it were their blood, and was spilled upon the ground. But Ungoliant sucked it up, and going then from Tree to Tree she set her black beak to their wounds, till they were drained; and the poison of Death that was in her went into their tissues and withered them, root, branch, and leaf; and they died... Ungoliant belched forth black vapours as she drank, and swelled to a shape so vast and hideous that Melkor was afraid" (Sil, 76).

47. "Then Fëanor swore a terrible oath. His seven sons leapt straightway to his side and took the selfsame vow together, and red as blood shone their drawn swords in the glare of the torches. They swore an oath which none shall break, and none should take, by the name even of Ilúvatar, calling the Everlasting Dark upon them if they kept it not; and Manwë they named in witness, and Varda, and the hallowed mountain of Taniquetil, vowing to pursue with vengeance and hatred to the ends of the World Vala, Demon, Elf or man as yet unborn, or any creature, great or small, good or evil, that time should bring forth unto the end of days, whoso should hold or take or keep a Silmaril from their possession" (83).

48. "There they beheld suddenly a dark figure standing high upon a rock that looked down upon the shore. Some say that it was Mandos himself, and no lesser herald of Manwë. And they heard a loud voice, solemn and terrible, that bade them stand and give ear. Then all halted and stood still, and from end to end of the hosts of the Noldor the voice was heard speaking the curse of prophecy which is called the Prophecy of the North, and the Doom of the Noldor" (87).

49. "Nothing did he known of Angband or the great strength of defence that Morgoth had so swiftly prepared; but even had he known it would not have deterred him, for he was fey, consumed by the flame of his own wrath. Thus it was that he drew far ahead of the van of his host; and seeing this the servants of Morgoth turn to bay, and there issued from

Angband Balrogs to aid them... At last [Fëanor] was smited to the ground by Gothmog, Lord of Balrogs, whom Ecthelion after slew in Gondolin" (107).

BIBLIOGRAPHY

Anderson, George K. *The Literature of the Anglo-Saxons*. Princeton: Princeton University Press, 1949.

Auden, W.H. "At the End of the Quest, Victory." *New York Times Book Review*, January 22, 1956, p.5.

Baker, Peter S., ed. *The Beowulf Reader*. New York: Garland Publishing, Inc., 2000.

Barber, Richard. *Myths & Legends of the British Isles*. Rochester: Boydell Press, 1999.

Barfield, Owen. *The Rediscovery of Meaning and Other Essays*. Middletown: Wesleyan University Press, 1977.

Barnfield, Marie. "Turin Turambar and the Tale of the Fostering." *Mallorn*. 31.December (1994): 29-36.

Barron, W.R.J. Trawthe and Treason: *The Sin of Gawain Reconsidered*. Manchester: Manchester University Press, 1980.

Beagle, Peter S. "Tolkien's Magic Ring." *Holiday*. 39.June (1966): 128,130,133-34.

Beatie, Bruce. "'Folk Tale, Fiction, and Saga in J.R.R. Tolkien's *The Lord of the Rings*." *Mankato State Studies*.2.February (1967): 1-17.

Becker, Alda, ed. *The Tolkien Scrapbook*. Philadelphia: Running Press, 1978.

Becker, Alda, ed. *The Tolkien Scrapbook*. New York: Grosset & Dunlap, 1978.

Beowulf. Edited and translated by R.M. Liuzza. Toronto: Broadview Literary Texts, 2000.

Bjork, Robert E., ed. *A Beowulf Handbook*. Lincoln: University of Nebraska Press, 1997.

Blissitt, William. "'Despots of the Ring'." *South Atlantic Quarterly*.

58.summer (1959): 448-456.
Bloom, Harold, ed. *Beowulf: Modern Critical Interpretations*. New York, Chelsea House Publishers, 1987.
Boswell, George W. "Tolkien as Litterateur." *South Central Bulletin*. 32.winter (1972): 188 -197.
Brewer, Elisabeth, ed. S*ir Gawain and the Green Knight: Sources and Analogues*. Rochester: Boydell & Brewer Ltd., 1992.
Campbell, Joseph. *The Hero with a Thousand Faces*. New York: Pantheon, 1949.
Carpenter, Humphrey. *The Inklings: C.S. Lewis, J.R.R. Tolkien, Charles Williams, and Their Friends*. Boston: Houghton Mifflin, 1979.
Carpenter, Humphrey. *Tolkien*. Boston: Houghton Mifflin Company, 1977.
Carpenter, Humphrey with Christopher Tolkien, ed. *The Letters of J.R.R. Tolkien*. Boston: Houghton Mifflin , 1981.
Carter, Lin. Tolkien: *A Look Behind 'The Lord of the Rings'*. New York: Ballantine, 1969.
Castell, Daphne. "The Realms of Tolkien." *New Worlds*. 50. November (1966): 143-54.
Cavill, P. "Interpretations of the Battle of Maldon lines 84-90." *Studia Neophilologica* 67 (1995) 149-64
Chance, Jane. *The Lord of the Rings: The Mythology of Power*. New York: Twayne, 1992.
Cherniss, Michael D. *Ingeld and Christ: Heroic Concepts and Values in Old English Christian Poetry*. The Hague: Mouton & Co., 1972.
Clark, George and Daniel Timmons, ed. *J.R.R. Tolkien and His Literary Resonances*. London: Greenwood Press, 2000.
Clein, Wendy. *Concepts of Chivalry in Sir Gawain and the Green Knight*. Norman: Pilgrim Books, 1987.
Crabbe, Katharyn. *J.R.R. Tolkien*. New York: Frederick Ungar, 1981.
Christensen, Bonniejean, '*Beowulf* and *The Hobbit*: Elegy into Fantasy in J.R.R. Tolkien's Creative Technique', *DAI*, 30 (1970) 4401A-4402A (University of Southern California).
Curry, Patrick. *Defending Middle-earth:Tolkien, Myth, and Modernity*. New York: St. Martin's Press, 1997.
Deutsch, Babette. *Hero's of the Kalevala: Finland's Saga*. New York: Julian Messner, Inc., 1940.
Dockery, Carl Dee, 'The Myth of Shadow in the Fantasies of Williams, Lewis, and Tolkien', *DAI*, 30 (1975) (Auburn University)
Dowie, William J. "Religious Fiction in a Profane Time: Charles Williams, C.S. Lewis, and J.R.R. Tolkien." Diss. Brandeis University, 1970.
Dronke, Ursula, ed. *The Poetic Edda Volume I Heroic Poems*. Oxford:

Clarendon Press, 1969.

DuBois, Thomas A. *Finnish Folk Poetry and the Kalevala*. New York: Garland Publishing, Inc., 1995.

Eirikr, Magnusson and William Morris. *The Story of the Volsungs & Niblungs*. London: George Prior Publishers, 1980.

Eliade, Mircea. *Cosmos and History: The Myth of Eternal Return*. New York: Harper & Row, 1959.

Elliot, Ralph W.V. "Byrhtnoth and Hildebrand: A Study of Heroic Technique." In *Studies in Old English Literature in Honor of Arthur G. Brodeurm*, edited by Stanley B. Greenfield, 53-70. Eugene: University of Oregon Books, 1963.

Ellwodd, Gracia Fay. *Goodness From Tolkien's Middle-earth: Two Essays on the "Applicability of The Lord of the Rings"*. Grand Rapids: Eerdmans Publishing Company, 1970.

Evans, Robley. *Writers For the Seventies: J.R.R. Tolkien*. New York: Thomas Y. Crowell Company, 1978.

Evans, Steven S. *The Heroic Poetry of Dark-Age Britain*. New York: University Press of America, Inc., 1997.

Evans, Steven S. *The Lords of Battle: Image and Reality of the Comitatus in Dark-Age Britain*. New York: The Boydell Press, 1997.

Evans, W.D. Emrys. *"The Lord of the Rings."* *The School Librarian*. 16.December (1968): 284-88.

Everett, Caroline Whitman, 'The Imaginative Fiction of J.R.R. Tolkien', (M.A. Florida State University, 1957).

Fajardo-Acosta, Fidel. *The Condemnation of Heroism in the Tragedy of Beowulf*. Queenstown, The Edwin Mellen Press, 1991.

Fletcher, George U. *The Well of the Unicorn*. New York: William Sloane Associates, Inc., 1948.

Flieger, Verlyn. *A Question of Time: J.R.R. Tolkien's Road to Faerie*. Kent, OH: Kent University Press, 1997.

Flieger, Verlyn. *Splintered Light: Logos and Language in Tolkien's World*. Grand Rapids: Wm. B. Eerdmans Publishing Company, 1983.

Flieger, Veryln and Carl F. Hostetter, ed. *Tolkien's Legendarium: Essays on The History of Middle-earth*. Westport, Connecticut and London: Greenwood Press, 2000.

Flieger, Veryln. "Taking the Part of Trees: Eco-Conflict in Middle-earth." In *J.R.R. Tolkien and His Literary Resonances: Views of Middle-earth*. Edited by George Clark and Daniel Timmons. London: Greenwood Press, 2000, pgs. 147-159.

Fonstad, Karen Wynn. *The Atlas of Middle-earth*. Boston: Houghton Mifflin, 1981 rev. 1998.

Foster, Robert. *Teacher's Guide to The Hobbit.* New York: Ballantine Books, 1981.
Foster, Robert. *A Guide to Middle-earth.* New York: Ballantine, 1971.
Fox, Denton, ed. *Twentieth Century Interpretations of Sir Gawain and the Green Knight.* Edgewood Cliffs, N.J.: Princeton-Hall, Inc., 1968.
Frantzen, Allen J. *Anglo-Saxonism and the Construction of Social Identity.* Gainesville: Fla. University Press, 1997.
Frazer, James G. *The Golden Bough.* New York: The MacMillan Co., 1927.
Frazer, Sir James George. *The Golden Bough.* New York: Stratford Press, Inc., 1922.
Frye, Northrop. *Fables of Identity: Studies in Poetic Mythology.* New York: Harcourt, Brace & World, Inc., 1963.
Frye, Northrop. *Anatomy of Criticism.* New York: Atheneum, 1967.
Gatch, Milton, McC. *Loyalties and Traditions: Man and His World in Old English Literature.* New York: The Bobbs-Merrill Company, Inc., 1971.
Giddings, Robert. *J.R.R. Tolkien: This Far Land.* Totowa, NJ: Barns and Noble, 1984.
Giddings, Robert and Elizabeth Holland. *J.R.R. Tolkien: The Stories of Middle-earth.* London: Junction Books, 1981.
Girvan, Ritchie. *Finnsburuh.* Oxford: Oxford University Press, 1941.
GoodKnight, Glen. "A Comparison of Cosmological Geography in the Works of J.R.R. Tolkien, C.S. Lewis, and Charles Williams." *Mythlore.* 1.July (1969): 18-22.
Gordon, E.V., ed. *The Battle of Maldon.* London: Methuen, 1937.
Green, William H. *The Hobbit: A Journey into Maturity.* New York: Twayne Publishers, 1995.
Green, William Howard, 'The *Hobbit* and Other Fiction by J.R.R. Tolkien: Their Roots in Medieval Heroic Literature and Language', *DAI*, 30 (1970) 4944A (Louisiana State University).
Grigson, Geoffrey, ed. *A Choice of William Morris's Verse.* London: The University Press Glasgow, 1969.
Grotta-Kurska, Daniel. *J.R.R. Tolkien: Architect of Middle Earth.* Philadelphia: Running Press, 1976.
Guest, Lady Charlotte. *The Mabinogion (The Red Book of Hergest).* London: John Jones Cardiff Ltd., 1877.
Haines, Victor Yelverton. *The Fortunate Fall of Sir Gawain: The Typology of Sir Gawain and the Green Knight.* New York: University Press of America, 1982.
Haggard, H. Rider. *She & King Solomon's Mines.* New York: Modern Library, 1957.
Haymes, Edward R. *The Nibelungenlied.* Chicago: University of Illinois

Press, 1986.

Helms, Randal. *Tolkien and the Silmarils*. Boston: Houghton Mifflin, 1981.

Helms, Randel. *Tolkien's World*. Boston: Houghton Mifflin Company, 1974.

Hermann, John P. *Allegories of War: Language and Violence in Old English Poetry*. Ann Arbor: The University of Michigan Press, 1989.

Hill, John M. *The Anglo-Saxon Warrior Ethic: Reconstructing Lordship in Early English Literature*. Tallahassee: University Press of Florida, 2000.

Hillegas, Mark R., ed. *Shadows of the Imagination: The Fantasies of C.S. Lewis, J.R.R. Tolkien*. Carbondale and Edwardsville: Illinois University Press, 1969.

Ogain, Daithi O. *The Hero in Irish Folk History*. New York: St. Martin's Press, 1985.

Hole, Christina. *English Folk-Heroes*. New York: B.T. Batsford, Ltd., 1948.

Howard, Green, William. *The Hobbit and Other Fiction by J.R.R. Tolkien: Their Roots in Medieval Heroic Literature and Language*. Place of Publication: Publisher, 1970.

Irwin, W.R. "There and back Again: The Romance of Williams, Lewis, and Tolkien." *Sewanee Review*. 69.fall (1961): 566-578.

Isaacs, Neil D., and Rose a Zimbardo, ed. *Tolkien and the Critics: Essays on J.R.R. Tolkien's The Lord of the Rings*. Notre Dame and London: University of Notre Dame Press, 1968.

Johnson, J.A. "'Farmer Giles of Ham: What is It?'." *Orcist*. 1.7 (1972-73): 21-4.

Johnson, Judith Ann. *J.R.R. Tolkien: Six Decades of Criticism*. Westport, CT: Greenwood Press, 1986.

Johnson, Lynn Stanley. *The Voice of the Gawain-Poet*. Madison: University of Wisconsin Press, 1984.

Kalevala: The Land of Heroes. Compiled by Elias Lonnrot. 1849. Translated by W. F. Kirby. London: J.M. Dent & Sons, 1907.

The Kalevala, or Poems of the Kalevala District. Compiled by Elias Lonnrot. A Prose Translation with Foreword and Appendices by Francis Peabody Magoun, Jr. Cambridge, Mass.: Harvard University Press, 1963.

Kennedy, Charles W. *The Earliest English Poetry*. New York: Oxford University Press, 1943.

Keynes, Geoffrey, ed. *Blake; Complete Writings*. London: Oxford University Press, 1966.

Kilby, Clyde. *Tolkien and the Silmarills*. Wheaton, Ill.: Harold Shaw, 1981.

Kirby, I.J. "In Defence of Byrhtnoth." In *Florilegium* volume 11 (1992).

Kirby, W.F. *Kalevala: The Land of Heroes*. London: J.M. Dent & Co., 1907.

Kocher, Paul H. *A Reader's Guide to The Silmarillion.* Boston: Houghton Mifflin Company, 1980.

Kocher, Paul H. *Master of Middle-earth: The Fiction of J.R.R. Tolkien.* Boston: Houghton Mifflin, 1972.

Lang, Andrew. *The Blue Fairy Book.* Philadelphia: Macrae Smith Company, Year.

Lettsom, William Nanson. *The Nibelungenlied.* New York: Charles Scribner's Sons, 1903.

Levitin, Alexis, "J.R.R. Tolkien's " (M.A., Columbia University, 1964).

Levitin, Alexis. "The Genre of *The Lord of the Rings.*" *Tolkien Journal.* 4.January (1970): 4-8, 22.

Liuzza, R.M. *Beowulf.* Ontario: Broadview Press Ltd., 2000.

Lobdell, Jared. ""The Tolkien Papers"." *Mankato Studies in English.* 2.February (1967).

Lobdell, Jared, ed. *A Tolkien Compass.* La Salle, Ill.: Open Court Press, 1975.

London, MG. "Lead, Follow, of Go Over the Sea." www.ssfworld.com, 2002.

Lynn, David H. *The Hero's Tale: Narrators in the Early Modern Novel.* London: The Macmillan Press Ltd, 1989.

MacDonald, George. *The Golden Key and the Green Life.* Suffolk: St Edmundsbury Press, 1986.

Magoun,, Francis Peabody, Jr., ed. *The Kalevala or Poems of the Kaleva District.* Cambridge: Harvard University Press, 1963.

Miesel, Sandra L. "'Some Motifs and Sources for Lord of the Rings'." *Riverside Quarterly.* 3 1968: 125-8.

Milton, John. *Paradise Lost.* London: S. Simmons, 1678.

Mitchison, Naomi. "One Ring to Bind Them." *New Statesman and Nation.* 48.September (1954): 331.

Morse, Robert E. *Evocation of Virgil in Tolkien's Art.* Oak Park, IL: Bolchazy-Carducci Publishers, 1986.

Morse, Robert. "From the Snake to the Caterpillar: The Influence of Vergil on J.R.R. Tolkien." *Classical Outlook.* November 1976.

Moseley, Charles. *Writers and Their Works: J.R.R. Tolkien.* Plymouth, UK: Northcote House Publishers, 1997.

Moss, Leonard. *The Excess of Heroism in Tragic Drama.* Gainesville: University Press of Florida, 2000.

Nitzsche, Jane Chance. *Tolkien's Art: A 'Mythology for England'.* New York: St. Martin's Press, 1979.

Noel, Ruth. *The Mythology of Middle-earth.* Boston: Houghton Mifflin Company, 1977.

Noel, Ruth S. *The Languages of Tolkien's Middle-earth*. Boston: Houghton Mifflin, 1980.

Norman, Philip. "'The Prevalence of Hobbits." *The New York Times Magazine*. 15 Jan. 1967: 30- 1,97,100,102.

Norwood, W.D. "Tolkien's Intention in *The Lord of the Rings*." *Mankato State Studies*. 2.February (1967): 18-24.

O'Faolain, Sean. *The Vanishing Hero*. Boston: Atlantic Monthly Press, 1956.

O'Neill, Timothy. *Tolkien and The Hobbit*. Boston: Houghton Mifflin Co., 1979.

O'Neill, Timothy R. *The Individuated Hobbit: Jung, Tolkien and the Archetypes of Middle-earth*. Boston: Houghton Mifflin Company, 1979.

Parker, Douglas. "Hwaet We Holbytla..." *Hudson Review*. 9.Winter (1956-57): 598-609.

Partridge, Brenda. "No Sex Please – We're Hobbits: The Construction of Female Sexuality in *The Lord of the Rings*." In *J.R.R. Tolkien: This Far Land*. Edited by Robert Giddings. London: Vision Press Ltd., 1983, pg. 179-199.

Pearce, Anne C. *One Ring to Bind Them All: Tolkien's Mythology*. University, AL: University of Alabama Press, 1979.

Pearce, Joseph. *Tolkien: Man and Myth*. London and San Francisco: HarperCollins & Ignatius Press, 1998.

Pentikainen, Juha Y. *Kalevala Mythology*. Indianapolis: Indiana University Press, 1989.

Petty, Anne C. *One Ring to Bind Them All: Tolkien's Mythology*. University of Alabama: The University of Alabama Press, 1979.

Petty, Anne Cotton. "The Creative Mythology of J.R.R. Tolkien: A Study of the Mythic Impulse." Diss. Florida State University, 1972.

Pope, John C., ed. *Eight Old English Poems*. New York: WW Norton & Company, 2001.

Purtill, Richard L. *J.R.R. Tolkien: Myth, Morality, and Religion*. San Francisco: Harper & Row, 1984.

Purtill, Richard. *Lord of the Elves and the Eldils: Fantasy and Philosophy in C.S. Lewis and J.R.R. Tolkien*. Grand Rapids: Zondervan , 1974.

Rank, Otto. *The Myth and Birth of a Hero*. New York: Robert Brunner, 1952.

Rauer, Christine. *Beowulf and the Dragon*. New York: Boydell & Brewer Ltd., 2000.

Ready, William. *The Tolkien Relationship: A Personal Inquiry*. Chicago: Henry Regnery Company, 1968.

Reckford, Kenneth J., 'Some Trees in Virgil and Tolkien.' In *Perspectives of*

Roman Poetry: A Classics Symposium, ed. G. Karl Galinsky. Austin and London: University of Texas Press, 1974.

Rogers, Deborah Champion Webster. *The Fictitious Characters of C.S. Lewis and J.R.R. Tolkien in Relation to Their Medieval Sources.* Diss. University of Wisconsin, 1972.

Rogers, Ivor and Deborah Rogers. *J.R.R. Tolkien: A Critical Biography.* New York: Hippocrene Books, 1980.

Rosebury, Brian. *Tolkien: A Critical Assessment.* New York: St. Martin's Press, 1992.

Rossi, Lee D. *The Politics of Fantasy: C.S. Lewis and J.R.R. Tolkien.* Ann Arbor: UMI Research Press, 1984.

Rodrigues, Louis J. *Three Anglo-Saxon Battle Poems.* Felinfach, Llanerch Publishers, 1996.

Sale, Roger. *Modern Heroism: Essays on D.H. Lawrence, William Empson and J.R.R. Tolkien.* Berkeley, Los Angeles, and London: University of California Press, 1973.

Salu, Mary and Robert T. Farrell, ed. *J.R.R. Tolkien: Scholar and Storyteller- Essays in Memoriam.* Ithaca: Cornell University Press, 1979.

Scagg, D.G. *The Battle of Maldon.* Oxford: Oxford University Press, 1991.

Schlobin, Roger C. "The Monsters Are Talismans and Transgressions: Tolkien and *Sir Gawain and the Green Knight.*" In *J.R.R. Tolkien and His Literary Resonances.* Edited by George Clark and Daniel Timmons. London: Greenwood Press, 2000, pgs. 71-83.

Schoolfield, George C., ed. *The Kalevala: Epic of the Finnish People.* Helsinki: Otava Publishing Company Ltd, 1988.

Segal, Robert A., ed. *Hero Myths.* Malden: Blackwell Publishers, 2000.

Sir Gawain and the Green Knight. Edited and translated by William Vantuono. New York: Garland Publishing, 1991.

Sister, Pauline C.S.M. "Mysticism in the Ring." *Tolkien Journal.* 2.November (1969): 12-14.

Shippey, T.A. "Boar and Badger: An Old English Heroic Antithesis?' In *Sources and Relationships: Studies in Honour of J.E.* , edited by Mary Collins, Jocelyn Price, and Andrew Hamer, 220-39. Leeds Studies in England, new series, vol. 16. 1985.

Shippey, T.A. *The Road to Middle-Earth.* Boston: George Allen & Unwin, 1982.

Shippey, Tom. *J.R.R. Tolkien: Author of the Century.* Boston: Houghton Mifflin, 2001.

Spenser, Edmund. *The Faerie Queene,* in *The Poetical Works of Edmund Spenser,* edited by J.C. Smith and E. deSelincourt, 1942.

Stanton, Michael N. *Hobbits, Elves, and Wizards: Exploring the Wonders and Worlds of J.R.R. Tolkien's The Lord of the Rings*. New York: Palgrave, 2001.

St. Clair, Gloria Ann Strange Slaughter, 'studies in the Sources of J.R.R. Tolkien's *The Lord of the Rings*', DAI, 30 (1970) 50001A (Oklahoma).

Steadman, John M. *Milton and the Paradoxes of Renaissance Heroism*. Baton Rouge: Louisiana State University Press, 1987.

Stimpson, Catherine. *J.R.R. Tolkien. Columbia Essays on Modern Writers*, no. 41. New York: Columbia University Press, 1969.

Strachey, Barbara. *Journeys of Frodo: An Atlas of J.R.R. Tolkien's The Lord of the Rings*. London: HarperCollins, 1998.

Straight, Michael. "Fantastic World of Professor Tolkien." *New Republic*. 134.January (1956): 24-26.

Sydenham, G. *England Before The Norman Conquest*. New York: Haskell House Publishers Ltd., 1972.

Taylor, Paul B. and W.H. Auden. *The Elder Edda: A Selection*. London: The University Press Glasgow, 1969.

Thomson, George H. "*The Lord of the Rings*: The Novel as Traditional Romance." *Wisconsin Studies in Contemporary Literature*. 1.8 (43-59): 43-59.

Tolkien, Christopher, ed. *Book of Lost Tales Part I*. Boston: George Allen & Unwin, 1983.

Tolkien, Christopher, ed. *The Book of Lost Tales Part II*. Boston: George Allen & Unwin, 1984.

Tolkien, Christopher, ed. *The Return of the Shadow*. Boston: Houghton Mifflin Company, 1988.

Tolkien, Christopher, ed. *Sauron Defeated*. Boston: Houghton Mifflin Company, 1992.

Tolkien, Christopher, ed. *The War of the Ring*. Boston: Houghton Mifflin Company, 1990.

Tolkien, Christopher, ed. *The Shaping of Middle-Earth*. Boston: Houghton Mifflin Company, 1986.

Tolkien, Christopher, ed. *The Lost Road and Other Writings*. Boston: Houghton Mifflin Company, 1987.

Tolkien, Christopher, ed. *Morgoth's Ring*. Boston: Houghton Mifflin Company, 1993.

Tolkien, Christopher, ed. *The Treason of Isengard*. Boston: Houghton Mifflin Company, 1989.

Tolkien, Christopher, ed. *The Peoples of Middle-Earth*. Boston: Houghton Mifflin Company, 1996.

Tolkien, Christopher, ed. *The War of the Jewels*. New York: Houghton

Mifflin Company, 1994.

Tolkien, Christopher, ed. *The Lays of Beleriand*. New York: Ballantine Books, 1985.

Tolkien, Christopher, ed. *Unfinished Tales of Númenor and Middle-earth*. Boston: Houghton Mifflin, 1980.

Tolkien, J.R.R. "Beowulf: The Monsters and the Critics." In *The Monsters and the Critics and Other Essays*. Edited by Christopher Tolkien. Boston: George Allen & Unwin, 1983, pg. 5 -49.

Tolkien, J.R.R. and E.V. Gordon. *Sir Gawain and the Green Knight*. Oxford: Calendon Press, 1925.

Tolkien, J.R.R. *The Adventures of Tom Bombadil*. Boston: Houghton Mifflin Company, 1962.

Tolkien, J.R.R. *The Book of Lost Tales Book Two*. Edited by Christopher Tolkien. New York: Ballantine Books, 1983.

Tolkien, J.R.R. *The Children of Húrin*. Edited by Christopher Tolkien. New York: Houghton Mifflin Company, 2007.

Tolkien, J.R.R. *The Fellowship of the Ring*. New York: Ballantine Books, 1954.

Tolkien, J.R.R. *The Hobbit*. New York: Ballantine Books, 1966.

Tolkien, J.R.R. "The Homecoming of Beorhtnoth Beorhnthelm's Son." In *The Tolkien Reader*. New York: Ballantine Books, 1966, pg. 1-27.

Tolkien, J.R.R. "Leaf by Niggle." In *The Tolkien Reader*. New York: Ballantine Books, 1966, pg. 100-120.

Tolkien, J.R.R. *Letters of J.R.R. Tolkien*. Edited by Humphrey Carpenter with the assistance of Christopher Tolkien. London: George Allen & Unwin, 1981.

Tolkien, J.R.R. *The Lord of the Rings*. New York: Ballantine Books, 1970.

Tolkien, J.R.R. *The Monsters and the Critics and Other Essays*. Boston: George Allen & Unwin, 1983.

Tolkien, J.R.R. "On Fairy Stories." In *The Tolkien Reader*. New York: Ballantine Books, 1966, pg. 29-100.

Tolkien, J.R.R. *The Return of the King*. New York: Ballantine Books, 1954.

Tolkien, J.R.R. *The Silmarillion*. Boston: Houghton Mifflin Company, 1978.

Tolkien, J.R.R. "Sir Gawain and the Green knight." In *The Monsters and the Critics and Other Essays*. Edited by Christopher Tolkien. Boston: George Allen & Unwin, 1983, pg. 72-109.

Tolkien, J.R.R. *Smith of Wootton Major*. Boston: Houghton Mifflin, 1967.

Tolkien, J.R.R. *The Tolkien Reader*. New York: Ballantine Books, 1966.

Tolkien, J.R.R. *Tree and Leaf*. Boston: Houghton Mifflin, 1965.

Tolkien, J.R.R. *The Two Towers*. New York: Ballantine Books, 1954.

Urang, Gunnar. *Shadows of Heaven: Religion and Fantasy in C.S. Lewis, Charles Williams, and J.R.R. Tolkien.* Philadelphia: Pilgrim Press, 1971.

Vantuono, William, ed. *Sir Gawain and the Green Knight.* New York: Garland Publishing, Inc., 1991.

Volsunga Saga: The Story of the Vosungs and Niblungs, translated by William Morris. 1870. With an introduction and glossary by Robert W. Gutman. New York: Collier Books, 1962.

Waye, Hammond,. *J.R.R. Tolkien: A Descriptive Bibliography.* New Castle, De: Oak Knoll Books, 1993.

Weinig, Sister Mary Anthony. "Images of Affirmation: Perspectives of the Fiction of Charles Williams, C.S. Lewis, and J.R.R. Tolkien." *The University of Portland Review.* 20.Spring (1969): 43-46.

West, Richard C. *Tolkien Criticism: An Annotated Checklist.* Kent, Ohio: Kent State University Press, 1970.

West, Richard C. "Turin's Ofermod: An Old English Theme in the Development of the Story of Turin." In *Tolkien's Legendarium: Essays on The History of Middle-earth.* Edited by Veryln Flieger and Carl F. Hostetter. London: Greenwood Press, 2000, pg. 233-245.

Zacher, Christian, ed. *Critical Studies of Sir Gawain and the Green Knight.* London: University of Notre Dame Press, 1968.

J.R.R. Tolkien
The Books, The Films, The Whole Cultural Phenomenon

by Jeremy Mark Robinson

A new critical study of J.R.R. Tolkien, creator of Middle-earth and author of *The Lord of the Rings, The Hobbit* and *The Silmarillion*, among other books.
This new critical study explores Tolkien's major writings (*The Lord of the Rings, The Hobbit, Beowulf: The Monster and the Critics, The Letters, The Silmarillion* and *The History of Middle-earth* volumes); Tolkien and fairy tales; the mythological, political and religious aspects of Tolkien's Middle-earth; the critics' response to Tolkien's fiction over the decades; the Tolkien industry (merchandizing, toys, role-playing games, posters, Tolkien societies, conferences and the like); Tolkien in visual and fantasy art; the cultural aspects of The Lord of the Rings (from the 1950s to the present); Tolkien's fiction's relationship with other fantasy fiction, such as C.S. Lewis and *Harry Potter*; and the TV, radio and film versions of Tolkien's books, including the 2001-03 Hollywood interpretations of *The Lord of the Rings*.
This new book draws on contemporary cultural theory and analysis and offers a sympathetic and illuminating (and sceptical) account of the Tolkien phenomenon. This book is designed to appeal to the general reader (and viewer) of Tolkien: it is written in a clear, jargon-free and easily-accessible style.

754pp   ISBN 1-86171-057-7   £25.00 / $37.50

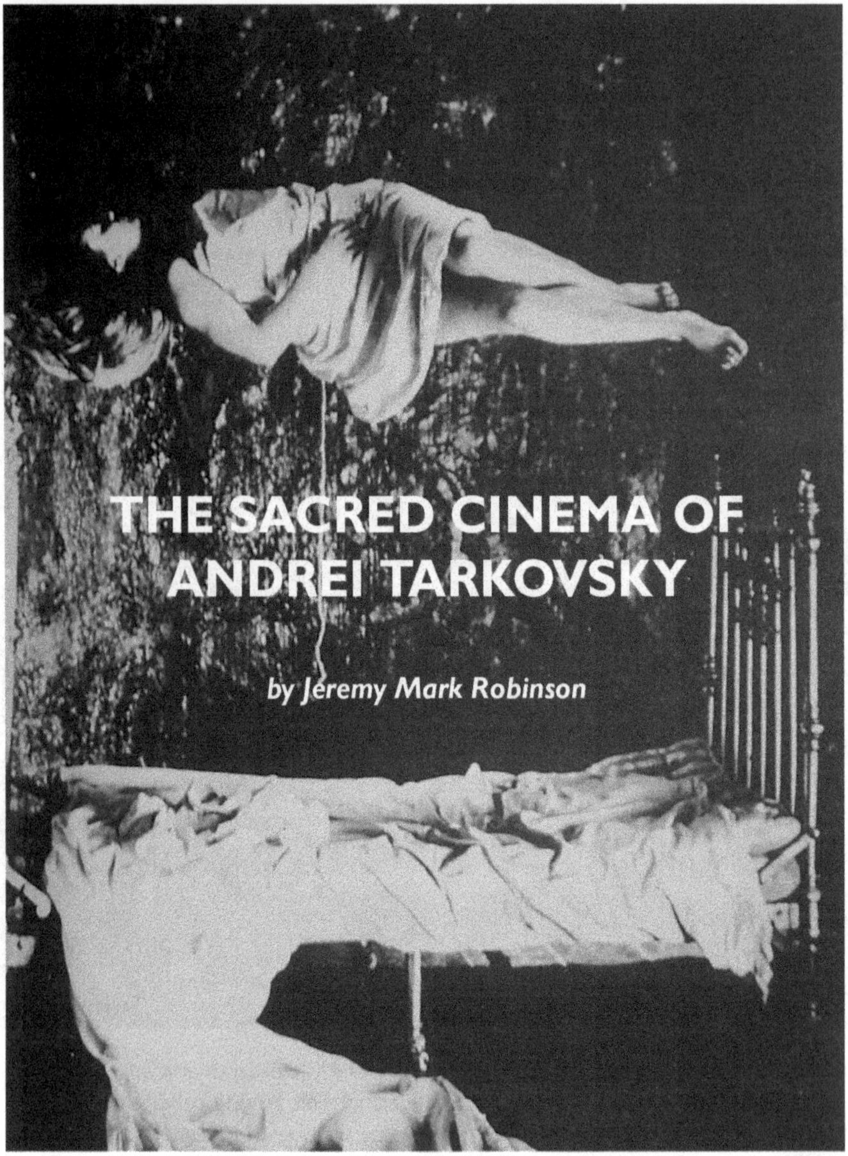

THE SACRED CINEMA OF ANDREI TARKOVSKY

by Jeremy Mark Robinson

A new study of the Russian filmmaker Andrei Tarkovsky (1932-1986), director of seven feature films, including *Andrei Roublyov, Mirror, Solaris, Stalker* and *The Sacrifice*.
This is one of the most comprehensive and detailed studies of Tarkovsky's cinema available. Every film is explored in depth, with scene-by-scene analyses. All aspects of Tarkovsky's output are critiqued, including editing, camera, staging, script, budget, collaborations, production, sound, music, performance and spirituality. Tarkovsky is placed with a European New Wave tradition of filmmaking, alongside directors like Ingmar Bergman, Carl Theodor Dreyer, Pier Paolo Pasolini and Robert Bresson.
An essential addition to film studies.

Illustrations: 150 b/w, 4 colour. 682 pages. First edition. Hardback.

Publisher: Crescent Moon Publishing. Distributor: Gardners Books.

ISBN 1-86171-096-8 (9781861710963) £60.00 / $105.00

The Best of Peter Redgrove's Poetry
The Book of Wonders

by Peter Redgrove, edited and introduced by Jeremy Robinson

Poems of wet shirts and 'wonder-awakening dresses'; honey, wasps and bees; orchards and apples; rivers, seas and tides; storms, rain, weather and clouds; waterworks; labyrinths; amazing perfumes; the Cornish landscape (Penzance, Perranporth, Falmouth, Boscastle, the Lizard and Scilly Isles); the sixth sense and 'extra-sensuous perception'; witchcraft; alchemical vessels and laboratories; yoga; menstruation; mines, minerals and stones; sand dunes; mud-baths; mythology; dreaming; vulvas; and lots of sex magic. This book gathers together poetry (and prose) from every stage of Redgrove's career, and every book. It includes pieces that have only appeared in small presses and magazines, and in uncollected form.

'Peter Redgrove is really an extraordinary poet' (George Szirtes, *Quarto* magazine)
'Peter Redgrove is one of the few significant poets now writing... His 'means' are indeed brilliant and delightful. Technically he is a poet essentially of brilliant and unexpected images...he never disappoints' (Kathleen Raine, *Temenos* magazine).

240pp   ISBN 1-86171-063-1   2nd edition   £19.99 / $29.50

Sex–Magic–Poetry–Cornwall
A Flood of Poems

by Peter Redgrove. Edited with an essay by Jeremy Robinson

A marvellous collection of poems by one of Britain's best but underrated poets, Peter Redgrove. This book brings together some of Redgrove's wildest and most passionate works, creating a 'flood' of poetry. Philip Hobsbaum called Redgrove 'the great poet of our time', while Angela Carter said: 'Redgrove's language can light up a page.' Redgrove ranks alongside Ted Hughes and Sylvia Plath. He is in every way a 'major poet'. Robinson's essay analyzes all of Redgrove's poetic work, including his use of sex magic, natural science, menstruation, psychology, myth, alchemy and feminism.
A new edition, including a new introduction, new preface and new bibliography.

'Robinson's enthusiasm is winning, and his perceptive readings are supported by a very useful bibliography' (*Acumen* magazine)
'*Sex-Magic-Poetry-Cornwall* is a very rich essay... It is like a brightly-lighted box. (Peter Redgrove)
'This is an excellent selection of poetry and an extensive essay on the themes and theories of this unusual poet by Jeremy Robinson' (*Chapman* magazine)

220pp   New, 3rd edition   ISBN 1-86171-070-4   £14.99 / $23.50

THE ART OF ANDY GOLDSWORTHY

COMPLETE WORKS: SPECIAL EDITION
(PAPERBACK and HARDBACK)

by William Malpas

A new, special edition of the study of the contemporary British sculptor, Andy Goldsworthy, including a new introduction, new bibliography and many new illustrations.

This is the most comprehensive, up-to-date, well-researched and in-depth account of Goldsworthy's art available anywhere.

Andy Goldsworthy makes land art. His sculpture is a sensitive, intuitive response to nature, light, time, growth, the seasons and the earth. Goldsworthy's environmental art is becoming ever more popular: 1993's art book *Stone* was a bestseller; the press raved about Goldsworthy taking over a number of London West End art galleries in 1994; during 1995 Goldsworthy designed a set of Royal Mail stamps and had a show at the British Museum. Malpas surveys all of Goldsworthy's art, and analyzes his relation with other land artists such as Robert Smithson, Walter de Maria, Richard Long and David Nash, and his place in the contemporary British art scene.

The Art of Andy Goldsworthy discusses all of Goldsworthy's important and recent exhibitions and books, including the *Sheepfolds* project; the TV documentaries; *Wood* (1996), the New York Holocaust memorial (2003); and Goldsworthy's collaboration on a dance performance.

Illustrations: 70 b/w, 1 colour. 330 pages. New, special, 2nd edition.
Publisher: Crescent Moon Publishing. Distributor: Gardners Books.

ISBN 1-86171-059-3 (9781861710598) (Paperback) £25.00 / $44.00

ISBN 1-86171-080-1 (9781861710802) (Hardback) £60.00 / $105.00

CRESCENT MOON PUBLISHING

ARTS, PAINTING, SCULPTURE

The Art of Andy Goldsworthy: Complete Works(Pbk)
The Art of Andy Goldsworthy: Complete Works (Hbk)
Andy Goldsworthy in Close-Up (Pbk)
Andy Goldsworthy in Close-Up (Hbk)
Land Art: A Complete Guide
Richard Long: The Art of Walking
The Art of Richard Long: Complete Works (Pbk)
The Art of Richard Long: Complete Works (Hbk)
Richard Long in Close-Up
Land Art In the UK
Land Art in Close-Up
Installation Art in Close-Up
Minimal Art and Artists In the 1960s and After
Colourfield Painting
Land Art DVD, TV documentary
Andy Goldsworthy DVD, TV documentary
The Erotic Object: Sexuality in Sculpture From Prehistory to the Present Day
Sex in Art: Pornography and Pleasure in Painting and Sculpture
Postwar Art
Sacred Gardens: The Garden in Myth, Religion and Art
Glorification: Religious Abstraction in Renaissance and 20th Century Art
Early Netherlandish Painting
Leonardo da Vinci
Piero della Francesca
Giovanni Bellini
Fra Angelico: Art and Religion in the Renaissance
Mark Rothko: The Art of Transcendence
Frank Stella: American Abstract Artist
Jasper Johns: Painting By Numbers
Brice Marden
Alison Wilding: The Embrace of Sculpture
Vincent van Gogh: Visionary Landscapes
Eric Gill: Nuptials of God
Constantin Brancusi: Sculpting the Essence of Things
Max Beckmann
Egon Schiele: Sex and Death In Purple Stockings
Delizioso Fotografico Fervore: Works In Process 1
Sacro Cuore: Works In Process 2
The Light Eternal: J.M.W. Turner
The Madonna Glorified: Karen Arthurs

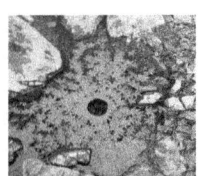

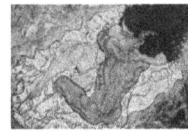

LITERATURE

J.R.R. Tolkien: The Books, The Films, The Whole Cultural Phenomenon
Harry Potter
Sexing Hardy: Thomas Hardy and Feminism
Thomas Hardy's *Tess of the d'Urbervilles*
Thomas Hardy's *Jude the Obscure*
Thomas Hardy: The Tragic Novels
Love and Tragedy: Thomas Hardy
The Poetry of Landscape in Hardy
Wessex Revisited: Thomas Hardy and John Cowper Powys
Wolfgang Iser: Essays
Petrarch, Dante and the Troubadours
Maurice Sendak and the Art of Children's Book Illustration
Andrea Dworkin
Cixous, Irigaray, Kristeva: The *Jouissance* of French Feminism
Julia Kristeva: Art, Love, Melancholy, Philosophy, Semiotics and Psychoanalysis
Hélene Cixous I Love You: The *Jouissance* of Writing
Luce Irigaray: Lips, Kissing, and the Politics of Sexual Difference
Peter Redgrove: Here Comes the Flood
Peter Redgrove: Sex-Magic-Poetry-Cornwall
Lawrence Durrell: Between Love and Death, East and West
Love, Culture & Poetry: Lawrence Durrell
Cavafy: Anatomy of a Soul
German Romantic Poetry: Goethe, Novalis, Heine, Hölderlin, Schlegel, Schiller
Feminism and Shakespeare
Shakespeare: Selected Sonnets
Shakespeare: Love, Poetry & Magic
The Passion of D.H. Lawrence
D.H. Lawrence: Symbolic Landscapes
D.H. Lawrence: Infinite Sensual Violence
Rimbaud: Arthur Rimbaud and the Magic of Poetry
The Ecstasies of John Cowper Powys
Sensualism and Mythology: The Wessex Novels of John Cowper Powys
Amorous Life: John Cowper Powys and the Manifestation of Affectivity (H.W. Fawkner)
Postmodern Powys: New Essays on John Cowper Powys (Joe Boulter)
Rethinking Powys: Critical Essays on John Cowper Powys
Paul Bowles & Bernardo Bertolucci
Rainer Maria Rilke
In the Dim Void: Samuel Beckett
Samuel Beckett Goes into the Silence
André Gide: Fiction and Fervour
Jackie Collins and the Blockbuster Novel
Blinded By Her Light: The Love-Poetry of Robert Graves
The Passion of Colours: Travels In Mediterranean Lands
Poetic Forms
The Dolphin-Boy

POETRY

The Best of Peter Redgrove's Poetry
Peter Redgrove: Here Comes The Flood
Peter Redgrove: Sex-Magic-Poetry-Cornwall
Ursula Le Guin: Walking In Cornwall
Dante: Selections From the Vita Nuova
Petrarch, Dante and the Troubadours
William Shakespeare: Selected Sonnets
Blinded By Her Light: The Love-Poetry of Robert Graves
Emily Dickinson: Selected Poems
Emily Brontë: Poems
Thomas Hardy: Selected Poems
Percy Bysshe Shelley: Poems
John Keats: Selected Poems
D.H. Lawrence: Selected Poems
Edmund Spenser: Poems
John Donne: Poems
Henry Vaughan: Poems
Sir Thomas Wyatt: Poems
Robert Herrick: Selected Poems
Rilke: Space, Essence and Angels in the Poetry of Rainer Maria Rilke
Rainer Maria Rilke: Selected Poems
Friedrich Hölderlin: Selected Poems
Arseny Tarkovsky: Selected Poems
Arthur Rimbaud: Selected Poems
Arthur Rimbaud: A Season in Hell
Arthur Rimbaud and the Magic of Poetry
D.J. Enright: By-Blows
Jeremy Reed: Brigitte's Blue Heart
Jeremy Reed: Claudia Schiffer's Red Shoes
Gorgeous Little Orpheus
Radiance: New Poems
Crescent Moon Book of Nature Poetry
Crescent Moon Book of Love Poetry
Crescent Moon Book of Mystical Poetry
Crescent Moon Book of Elizabethan Love Poetry
Crescent Moon Book of Metaphysical Poetry
Crescent Moon Book of Romantic Poetry
Pagan America: New American Poetry

MEDIA, CINEMA, FEMINISM and CULTURAL STUDIES

J.R.R. Tolkien: The Books, The Films, The Whole Cultural Phenomenon
Harry Potter
Cixous, Irigaray, Kristeva: The *Jouissance* of French Feminism
Julia Kristeva: Art, Love, Melancholy, Philosophy, Semiotics and Psychoanalysis
Luce Irigaray: Lips, Kissing, and the Politics of Sexual Difference
Hélene Cixous I Love You: The *Jouissance* of Writing
Andrea Dworkin
'Cosmo Woman': The World of Women's Magazines
Women in Pop Music
Discovering the Goddess (Geoffrey Ashe)
The Poetry of Cinema
The Sacred Cinema of Andrei Tarkovsky (Pbk and Hbk)
Paul Bowles & Bernardo Bertolucci
Media Hell: Radio, TV and the Press
An Open Letter to the BBC
Detonation Britain: Nuclear War in the UK
Feminism and Shakespeare
Wild Zones: Pornography, Art and Feminism
Sex in Art: Pornography and Pleasure in Painting and Sculpture
Sexing Hardy: Thomas Hardy and Feminism

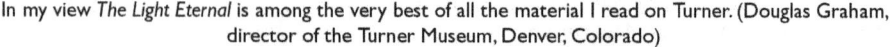

In my view *The Light Eternal* is among the very best of all the material I read on Turner. (Douglas Graham, director of the Turner Museum, Denver, Colorado)

The Light Eternal is a model monograph, an exemplary job. The subject matter of the book is beautifully organised and dead on beam. (Lawrence Durrell)

It is amazing for me to see my work treated with such passion and respect. (Andrea Dworkin)

Sex-Magic-Poetry-Cornwall is a very rich essay... It is like a brightly-lighted box. (Peter Redgrove)

CRESCENT MOON PUBLISHING
P.O. Box 393, Maidstone, Kent, ME14 5XU, United Kingdom.
01622-729593 (UK) 01144-1622-729593 (US) 0044-1622-729593 (other territories)
cresmopub@yahoo.co.uk   www.crescentmoon.org.uk

www.ingramcontent.com/pod-product-compliance
Lightning Source LLC
Chambersburg PA
CBHW062226080426
42734CB00010B/2037